Gifts from Ascended Beings of Light

Prayers, Meditations, Mantras and Journeys for Soul Growth

By Nasrin Safai
with Victoria A. Kaharl

Agapi

Library of Congress Control Number 2003112476
ISBN 0-974-5058-0-3

Published by AGAPI
Cover photo by Don Farrall from Elements 2
Cover design and typography by Kathleen A. Speers

You can order this book by calling 1-800-247-6553.
Address all inquiries to gifts@nasrinsafai.com, or visit www.nasrinsafai.com.

This is for you, for the divine being of light that you are.

And this is for all the ascended beings of light who
have offered gifts of love, wisdom and healing.

You are the light of the world...
the Kingdom of God is within you.

- Jesus (Matthew 5:14, Luke 17:21)

Contents

Introduction

Gifts of unconditional love await you in the pages of this book, in the words and the energies attached to every letter and every thought that went into making these offerings and making them available to you.

This book is a product of divine intention. Although the ascended master Jesus does not have a chapter in this book, he is the one who requested that Victoria and I put this book together and, as it turned out, his words begin this book and appear elsewhere through it.

All of the ascended beings included in this book chose to be here. All of the channeled material came through me, Nasrin. For the most part, this material is recent, some of it channeled in workshops or sacred ceremonies or to me alone in the privacy of my own home or in remote areas of the world or in cities, towns, villages, even uninhabited fields and plains, from Cape Town, South Africa to Cambridge Bay on the Arctic Circle and from the Gobi Desert in Mongolia to Kilauea volcano in Hawaii.

Ascended beings are known to people everywhere. They may be called saints or archangels or ascended masters or something else. Among perhaps the most well known in the West are Jesus and his mother Mary, and in the East, Buddha and Quan Yin. Many of them who speak from these pages can be found in the sacred literature of the world's major religions— Christianity, Islam, Judaism, Buddhism, and Hinduism.

In this book, however, none of the ascended beings discusses religion. They do address spirituality, which is quite another matter.

Their message is the same, repeated in different ways and in different styles, according to who the messenger is. The ascended master Quan Yin *invites* us to put aside our anger and open our hearts. All tell us to head for the light; Hecate urges us to *run* for it. Metatron, sounding almost exasperated, says he will do *whatever it takes* to make us see the path of light. Buddha insists that we must work harder to hold the energies of peace and nonviolence.

As remote as these enlightened beings might seem, each has a distinct personality. They are just as real as you and I, just as uniquely different as you and I, as you and your brother or mother or spouse.

They not only sound different from one another, but they also look and feel different. I am one of those who can see and hear and communicate with ascended beings who are constantly present among us but invisible to most of us. For as long as I can remember, I have asked to serve these beings of light and almost 20 years ago, I dedicated my life to bringing their messages and making their guidance available to those who desire it.

All of the enlightened beings in this book remind us what we have forgotten— that we are divine, that we are a part of God, that God is within each of us.

They tell us again and again to call on them for help because they can help us only if we request assistance. We must request the help to receive it because ours is a free-will planet.

It doesn't matter what religion or faith we may profess. All that matters is that we are sincere about our spirituality and our desire for the light— to go to the light, to stay in the light and to spread the light, the Light of God.

One lesson I have learned well is that there is only one God. You might dress him or her up, but this is still the one and only God.

I have made my home, at different times in my life, on three continents. I was born in Teheran, Iran. I lived my constructive young adult years in Europe and then moved to the United States, which I have called home for some 20 years. I am still the devout Shiite Muslim of my childhood and adolescence. I am also the devout Buddhist of my young adulthood. In the most troubled years of mid-life, I found Jesus and Mary who offered me the solace I craved. I have also evolved spiritually through Hindu scriptures and practices.

I hold space for the eastern ways and the western ways. I can see the best in both worlds and for that I am grateful. Initially, however, it was not easy to straddle both worlds. Why did God have me born in the Middle East when I would move to the West? If I were to live among people of all religions, why was I raised Muslim?

I don't ask such questions anymore. In fact I am grateful for where my life has taken me. Along the way of my path, I have seen how people of different worlds, different cultures, and different religions have come together by setting aside their differences, whatever they are, and working together, even praying together— especially praying.

This is often repeated by the holy beings in this book— that it is time for us to truly see every human being as a citizen of a single united world. This same message has been repeated throughout the ages, not in the least by the ascended master Jesus, who said: *I tell you the truth, whatever you did for one of the least of my brothers you did for me.* (Matthew 25:40)

The point, as excruciatingly simple as it is, is about love. This is the point: All is one. Do unto others, as you would have them do unto you. God is in me and God is in you. If you are angry with God, the supreme consciousness, your anger will affect your relationships with others. How can it not?

Besides their messages of love and God unity, these special beings of light also suggest prayers, meditations, mantras and other exercises for spiritual growth and healing.

Technically, a mantra is a series of sacred syllables or words or both. But in this book, the ascended beings use mantra interchangeably with prayer.

If prayer is talking to God and meditation is listening, chanting a mantra is preparing the mind and the body for the musical connection of both.

Until now, none of this channeled material has been made public. For my first seven years in this field, I was not permitted to even tape record any of my channelings. And sometimes when someone did try to tape record a channeling, the tape would be empty.

There are four discourses in this book that mark the beginning of my recorded archives. These are from Hecate, Lakshmi, Melchizedek and Quan Yin; they were channeled on the same day, October 28, 1997.

These first channelings that I was permitted to tape record were channeled when I was in beloved Satya Sai Baba's ashram in Puttaparthi, Indian. Sai Baba is a living saint who receives multitudes of people from around the globe on a daily basis.

I went to India because in a vision, Sai Baba called to me to spend a month at his ashram attending his birthday celebration in 1997. Before my departure, he rewarded me with a great gift. He instructed me to bring a tape recorder because during my stay, material would be given to me that would be included in books.

This material was channeled in a garden on the ashram grounds or my room. While the ascended beings I channeled are clearly speaking to an audience of more than one, I was alone during these channelings.

In the privacy of my dorm room, I was not self-conscious, but in the garden, where I was instructed (by divine guidance) to be, I felt quite silly. All I could think was that here I was with my eyes shut in meditation and my mouth moving and a tape recorder going and what would someone walking by think?

But soon I became lost in the energy that engulfed me. I was where I usually am when I channel. A part of me hovers somewhere above my head; another part of me seems to be on my right shoulder listening; another part of me is at my left shoulder watching; and another part of me is somehow a part of the ascended being I am channeling because I see through that being's eyes.

More and more of us are awakening to our own spirituality. Increasingly more of us are coming to the same inexorable conclusion that we are not alone and that time, as Melchizedek says, is of the essence in getting our act together. *You must clean your planet,* he says, *your spirit bodies, your physical bodies, your emotional bodies.*

When a master offers such gifts as an initiation or a journey or a healing, as they do in these pages, they do it out of love for us and only when they feel that we truly desire to receive such gifts. When an ascended being in these pages takes you on a journey or teaches you to use an energetic tool to reconnect to your own source, you are not simply reading about these activities. If you are a truly willing participant, that holy being is in your living room with you, taking you by the hand, guiding you and making sure you receive the benefit of what has been promised, whether it is a healing or simple words of wisdom.

You may not see or hear that being or sense that energy, but as long as you actively participate, the energies are there. Remember that the energy of a single thought is just as powerful as the energy of a spoken word or an action.

Remember, too, that you have only to call on these ascended beings. They have promised that when you call, they will answer. The connection is instantaneous.

Metatron offers some suggestions about our participation. "When you say these mantras," he says, "you embody yourself with the illumination of the I Am That I Am. You bring forth life in the purest and most innocent essence. You bring the divinity of the Godhead into your body; you embody that divinity. When you say your affirmations, you must believe them, so much so that nothing can make you take your eyes away from the presence of the I AM. Say it from your heart. Say it from your mind. Most importantly, say it from your gut, that part of your being that knows right and wrong."

Before you begin to pray or meditate or journey with an ascended being of light, prepare yourself. Invoke the I Am Presence— that is, the I AM That I AM— that resides within each of us. When you do this, you are bringing to yourself the supreme and loving power of God in action.

***God said to Moses, 'I AM WHO I AM.
This is what you say to the Israelites:
'I AM has sent me to you.'***

- Bible, Exodus 2:14

Buddha

Lord Buddha is most famous for founding the Buddhist religion. As Siddhartha Shakyamuni, he was born to royalty in 624 BC in what is now Nepal. As a young man, he was deeply moved to see for the first time the suffering of poverty, sickness, old age and hunger outside the palace walls.

The compassion he felt developed into a resolve to help people by freeing them from the karmic cycle of suffering. But he realized that in order to do this, he needed the wisdom of enlightenment. He left his home in search of it. After years of meditating, he became a fully enlightened being— that is to say, he realized the Godself within him as himself.

Followers of Buddha who have achieved enlightenment through offering themselves in similar service to the light are known as bodhisattvas. Quan Yin is a bodhisattva of compassion.

Lord Buddha has offered many aspects of himself in assistance to humankind. Each of these aspects carries specific qualities and thus, there are many Buddhas representing each quality. In the course of this book, you will come across invocations calling upon Buddhas and bodhisattvas of compassion and other qualities.

Buddha has incarnated in human embodiment 14 times to rescue humankind from pain and suffering and to teach compassion. The Dalai Lama, the Spiritual Master and Leader of Tibet, is the current and fourteenth incarnation of Buddha.

The thirteenth Buddha was part of the reason I found myself in the Gobi Desert in the winter of 2000, wondering which direction to head in.

My spirit guides, all ascended beings of light, had asked me to go to Mongolia to anchor the energies of the etheric or energetic

Shamballa (Heaven), to in effect bring back these energies. (At one time, Heaven— as Paradise or the Garden or Eden— existed on Earth.)

I knew others had done this in other areas but my guide (Metatron) said this would be different— there were certain energies he wanted anchored in a certain format and I was to do this with 12 other people because there had to be 13 of us who performed this ritual to raise the vibrations. Metatron also said we had to do this in February.

So I led a group of 16 from the U.S. to Mongolia. It was bitterly cold— temperatures far below freezing. By the time we got to Ulaan Baatar, the capital, there were only 10 of us; others had dropped out along the way for one reason or another.

We now faced the challenge of getting to the upper Gobi. We could hire a bus, which would take two days. Or we could take converted Russian tanks, another very long trip. I chose the only other option available but the shortest— an old Russian helicopter that looked as if it had seen plenty of action in a war. With a stop for fuel, the chopper ride would be eight hours one way.

Exactly where we were going— other than to the upper Gobi Desert— I didn't know. I knew that our ceremony had to be performed before sunset on this day.

When the helicopter landed, the sun was about a half hour from setting, and there were Jeeps waiting to take us further on this journey— a three-hour ride across the desert to the sand dunes, which were the major tourist attraction.

But a three-hour ride was out of the question if we were to do our ceremony before darkness fell. My guidance also included the warning that none of us should be exposed to the outside temperature for more than a half hour at a time. It was 40 degrees Fahrenheit *below* zero.

We had made it this far, I thought, now what?

I asked our interpreter and guide if there was a sacred site nearby. She had to think about this. Finally, she said yes, there was a sacred site.

Obviously tourists to the area don't usually have this sacred site on their itinerary— whatever it was. She didn't say.

It was almost sunset when we reached the sacred site. It was a very small shrine, a stupa that was perhaps large enough for one person to kneel inside and make an offering of incense and prayers.

The 10 of us in my group gathered in a circle around the shrine, and I prayed that this energy could be anchored with less people than the required 13.

Just then, the caretakers of the shrine, a husband and wife, came to greet us and asked if they could participate in our ceremony. Now we were 12 and with our translator— necessary to translate our prayer for the caretakers— we were 13.

We prayed— the prayer that my spirit guides gave me— "that in the name of the Twelve and the One, free Shamballa from the heavens and bring it to Earth."

My guides had never explained who the "Twelve and the One" were; nor had I asked. By now, I had been saying this prayer for the past nine months in different places all around the world.

When we finished the prayer, the sun was at the horizon. I asked our interpreter what the significance of this small shrine was. She said this was the exact birthplace of the thirteenth Dalai Lama— that is, the thirteenth reincarnation of Buddha.

Now I knew— the Twelve and the One were all Buddhas. I later discovered that Shamballa is the etheric seat of Lord Buddha.

(The mantra for the return of Shamballa is in the Metatron section.)

Rethinking a Future of Nonviolence

Buddha, channeled May 14, 2003

If you have to be the one who holds the rifle or the one that is the victim, which one would you choose?

My dearly beloveds, I am Buddha. For a period of five years I have a great dispensation to hold the energies of nonviolence over Earth and humanity. The year 2000 was the beginning of this dispensation.

The Weasak Festival of 2000 brought with it a great many cherished and blessed events. The birthday of Buddha is known as the Festival of Weasak and it happens to fall in the same month as the month of our blessed divine mother, Mother Mary.

In this month of May 2003, as we come together to offer you our blessings, I say to you that together we have two more years to build upon this special vibration that I have holding upon your planet. This vibration is the vibration of nonviolence—nonviolence and compassion.

I understand that as I speak these words, your mind may be moved to think of all the violent events that have taken place ever since my reign on the Ray of Nonviolence. And it will be justified for you to ask me that: How is it possible that if you are given the Ray of Nonviolence since May of 2000, and here we are May of 2003, so many violent manmade and natural disasters have hit Earth and humankind?

My answer would be: Imagine what could have happened had I not been given this dispensation, had I not been holding the energies of nonviolence over your heads like a blanket of light over your planet. Imagine the degree of violence that could hit you. Imagine how much of this violence I have assisted in diffusing. Imagine if I were to tell you what you have experienced is perhaps less than five percent of what you could have experienced had I not been given this dispensation since May of 2000.

And here we are three years into this course, three-fifths into its completion, and we are getting many violent disasters— natural, in the form of floods, volcanoes, hurricanes, typhoons and so forth, and manmade, in the form of wars and trespassing amongst human beings, whether it be violence against children, violence against one another, assault and battery amongst family members, violence in the streets of all different countries, violence imposed by one race against another, one nation against another, intentions of violence, actions of violence, thoughts of violence.

Imagine if you had to multiply this by 95 percent. And imagine that we are three-fifths into this cycle. We have two-fifths of the cycle left.

We must work harder to hold out the energies of nonviolence like an umbrella of light over the planet, over the continents, over the countries, over our towns and cities, over our villages, over our street corners, inside the houses, within the family members' hearts.

We must go into the peace and light of nonviolence. We must observe and exercise and propagate the peace and light of nonviolence.

We must begin to rethink our future, the future of our children, the future of our countries, the future of our nations, the future of our continents, the future of our world. We must rethink our future as one globe, one world, one being, one heartbeat, one life force, one light, one light returning to its source as pure white light.

I am here to offer you the energies of nonviolence.

There are Buddhas and bodhisattvas of compassion offering vigilant prayer, discourses, and invocations to bring the illumination of light to offer energies of nonviolence, to become beacons of light, illuminating and transmitting the vibration of nonviolence.

It is time for your mother planet to shake herself off of all violent energies.

What that means is whatever violence has been absorbed by her surface, by her heart core, by her skin, by her body, by her organs, is now coming to the surface to be released. As it comes to the surface, much like the pain that comes to the surface of your body, you will feel it.

As it comes to the surface to be released, that violence will be experienced in the street corner between two brothers. That violence will be experienced between a husband and wife. That violence will be experienced by a mother to her unborn child. That violence will be experienced by a father to his toddler, infant, child or the child of a friend or neighbor. That violence will be experienced through floods, hurricanes, typhoons, volcanic eruptions, earthquakes and other natural disasters because that violence is coming to the surface.

Just as a boil on the surface of your skin has to come to its pus and the pus has to break until it is released from the surface of the skin until the skin can heal itself, this violence has to come to the surface and the atmosphere and the body of Mother Earth in the form of natural disasters.

This violence has to come from the heart core of your emotional body to the surface of your body. Verbal conflict is the result. If verbal conflict does not suffice, some of you will take more violent action, going from verbal to physical harm, harm that might even take lives. This is part of the process.

To curb this process, you must constantly and continuously be antennas of light vibrating nonviolence. Just as the violet transmutational fire is the light that sheds its transmutational forces, absorbing to itself the darkness, you must send out nonviolent thoughts, nonviolent prayers, nonviolent invocations, beaming from your own body, using your body as a beacon, sending out nonviolence so that you can absorb to yourself and transmute into the light those violent thoughts, those angry thoughts of the angry people around you.

Do not join the anger, even when you feel righteous. If you are demonstrating for peace, make it a peaceful demonstration. How does a peace demonstration that ends in violence help the peace?

Ask yourself that question. How does a peace demonstration that ends up in assault and battery help nonviolence? How does your desire to act nonviolently serve itself if you raise the anger or the opposition of others that leads to violent actions that are used against you?

Are you in any way responsible when a violent reaction is directed to you? Is it possible that if you had not instigated the violence, you would not be at the receiving end of it? Is it possible that instead of being a mirror and sending back that violence, you could be a sponge and absorb the violence and transmute it in golden white light, in pure white light? Which one is more effective?

If you have to choose one out of the two, choose the sponge. But if you have to choose between being the mirror or the one holding the baton in the mirror, then just be the mirror.

If you have to be the one who holds the rifle or the one that is the victim, which one would you choose?

Mahatma Gandhi was a holy, sainted ascended master of light who came to Earth to anchor the energies of nonviolence. In the course of his lifetime, he was tested, pried and prodded with violent energies everywhere he went. He maintained his poise in nonviolence. His death scene was a testimony to the proof of his purpose. He attained with glory the victory of the service that he had brought as his offering to Earth. Remember him as a role model.

Lord Master Jesus brought the energies of divine love to Earth. His life and his crucifixion is a testimony to all the testing, prying and prodding that he went through throughout his life, even to his death. He succeeded in anchoring the energies of divine love and nonviolence.

Mother Teresa is another testimony. Princess Diana is another testimony. Quan Yin is another testimony. Mother Mary is another testimony to nonviolence, to divine love, to prayer, invocation and the awakening of the light. Use them as your role models.

Open your hearts and your homes to the presence of Lord

Buddha and the energies of nonviolence. Let Buddha sit facing your entranceway, your doorway, so that Buddha can send a prayer of nonviolence to everyone's heart who chooses to enter your home. Face a small statue of Buddha on your desk facing outside. Let Buddha with his surrender and nonviolence face your world, your career, your external world and transmute conflict and bring to you the cleared and cleansed forces of nonviolence.

Take Buddha with you in a small pouch where you go when you need to take steps and measures in the hopes of changing the world for better. During ceremony and ritual, let Buddha sit with you in your ceremonies. Invoke the presence of Buddha and bodhisattvas of compassion so that together we can hold the energies of compassion and nonviolence.

It is not through violence, it is no longer through an eye for an eye that we will attain ascension.

We will attain ascension when we can deflect the anger of another to the point that they will put their gun away, to the point that they will put their knife away, to the point that the power of our love diffuses their need to be violent.

Become powerful in your love for humanity and the world. Become powerful in shining your light and your nonviolence upon the world so that the world can learn from you and use you as a role model.

As the beacons of light, hold the light in nonviolence. And to practice this until you become perfect, call upon the Buddhas and bodhisattvas of compassion to assist you in the process.

With great love, I offer you my heart of nonviolence. I offer you my hand in assistance to diffuse violence. I am Buddha.

Mother Mary

The Ascended Master Mother Mary is best known as the mother of Jesus Christ. She is also called the Blessed Virgin Mary, the Madonna, the Queen of Heaven and the Installer of Peace on Earth. Mary says that Archangel Raphael is in her lineage of light, which makes her of the angelic realm.

Mother Mary represents the female force or polarity for the Western world, just as Quan Yin represents the same force for the East. Mother Mary is also well known to Muslims as Maryam or Mariam. Mary has her own surah or chapter (number 19) in the Qu'ran (or Koran) that relates the story of the birth of Jesus.

Mary has been making appearances for some 2000 years, ever since the end of her lifetime on Earth as the mother of Jesus. Over the course of the years, she has appeared to millions of people, sometimes initially only to children, as at Lourdes, France in 1858, and Chousa Velha near Fatima, Portugal, in 1916-17.

She has made many other appearances in Europe, and Africa, in North, South and Central America, Asia and the Middle East. From 1968-1971, she appeared hovering above the Coptic Orthodox Church of St. Mary's in Zeitoun near Cairo, Egypt. She made appearances in Kibeho, Rwanda from 1981-1989; in Vietnam in 1998; Akita, Japan in 1973. She first appeared in Medjugorje, Bosnia-Herzegovina in 1981 and she is still appearing there. The list goes on and on.

Her message after all these many years is steadfast: *Pray.*

Only Mother Mary really knows how often and where and to whom she is making her presence known.

When Ray Skop was 15 years old, he found a painting of the

Blessed Mother Mary and her mother Anne beside a dumpster in Jersey City, New Jersey. The dumpster was being filled with the demolition material of a house that was being torn down.

The painting was on a piece of tin about two feet long and a foot wide. Mary is depicted as a girl standing next to Anne.

Ray took the painting home. "Values are different now," he says. "In those days, you didn't leave a religious picture by the wayside. I gave it to my mother. She hung it up."

Over the years, the painting was kept in his parents' home or his home. In October of 1998, Ray noticed a substance dripping from the eyes of Mary and Saint Anne in the painting. On Good Friday of the following year, Ray exhibited the first signs of the stigmata. He began to bleed.

Ray has worked for many years in law enforcement. He is an investigator with the New Jersey prosecutor's office. Deeni Saltarelli, who knows him well, says, "He was a rough and tough type of dude and then the painting started weeping and then Mary came to him and asked him to get people to say the rosary. He never said the rosary before."

In time, crucifixes placed near the painting started to bleed. The back of the painting has also exhibited pictures— a crying Jesus, Jesus on the cross with two other crucifixes.

The substance that is "wept" from the painting has been analyzed. "It's like an olive oil," Ray says. "But a part of it, they couldn't come up with what it is. We all know Jesus healed with olive oil."

Ray shares the oil substance with anyone who requests it. Many people have been healed by the oil and Ray.

The reciting of the rosary, which started out monthly at the home of Ray and his wife Nancy, is done twice a week, every Friday and Wednesday.

Deeni found out about Ray in 1999 when her daughter's pediatrician suggested she go see him. Neither the pediatrician nor any other physician had been able to determine why Deeni's 27-month old daughter Samantha Rose had suddenly stopped walking.

Deeni managed to contact Ray by telephone and told him her story. He told her to bring Samantha Rose to the next rosary session.

"There were about 150 people outside his house when we got there," Deeni says. "Ray said to me, 'You'— He'd never seen me before— 'You come with me.' He said, 'Promise me you'll say the rosary every week for the rest of your life and your daughter will walk this weekend.' My heart was pounding so hard. The rosary? I could do that."

Deeni shared this with a few friends in the town where she lives in New Jersey but they were skeptical. "Everybody looked at me and said, 'Oh, my gosh, how can this man say this to you?' They thought it was crazy. I was just praying, Jesus, Mary, if you're there, help me."

That weekend on a Sunday, Samantha Rose told her mother she wanted to walk. Deeni held her up and Samantha Rose tried but could not walk. But she persisted. Again she said, "Mommy, I want to walk."

Again her mother held her up. "Within two or three minutes, her body lifted away from mine," Deeni says. "And in a few more minutes, she was walking all over the house and then she was running."

"I've witnessed many miracles from this man," Deeni says. "He's a very blessed man. He suffers. He's in a lot of pain with the stigmata. My mother once asked him, 'What do you call yourself— a healer?' He said, 'Ray, I'm just Ray.'"

Ray, now 55, is still an investigator with the New Jersey prosecutor's office. "I'm in the courtroom all day long five days a week," he says. "I've got three-quarters of the judicial system attending my rosaries."

In 2000 he established the Ray of Hope Foundation to help needy children in the area, including the underprivileged and those with debilitating illnesses (www.rayofhopefoundation.com).

Pray, Pray, Pray

Mother Mary, channeled May 14, 2003

Pray for the light to come to Earth.
Pray for the light to stay on Earth...

Pray for yourselves. Pray for your loved ones.
Pray for your enemies ten times more...

My children of light, I am Mary, your mother. My children, I ask you to pray. Pray, pray and pray. Pray for the light to come to Earth. Pray for the light to stay on Earth.

Pray for the light to open the hearts of all mankind, of all humanity, of all beings, of all souls, of all created and manifested spirit beings. Pray for the spirit of God to enter into the bodies of all souls. Pray for the heart of God to fill the hearts of all souls with light and love, with joy and happiness.

I come to bring you the news that your prayers are now received and magnified a thousand fold by my own prayers. As each one of you prays and joins me, that which you offer to the world in your prayers and invocations will be multiplied by a thousand fold merely by invoking your mother Mary to join you.

As you pray, even if that prayer is a simple conversation with God, with Mary, with ascended masters and mistresses, with gods and goddesses or directly with the throne of the Undifferentiated Source, call upon us to multiply and magnify your prayers and your conversations by a thousand fold, by ten thousand fold, by a hundred thousand fold, because this dispensation has been given to us to assist you in every way we can to multiply and magnify the good that you offer to the world.

Doing good can be in small increments.

Doing good can start from you being good to yourselves, from you being kind to yourselves, from you being gentle with yourselves, from you being loving to yourselves, from being worthy of love, from giving yourself permission to be worthy of love.

Many of you have said to me time and time again: "But this intention is not worthy of calling upon you. Why would I want to call you for something this simple or this trivial? How could I consider myself worthy of something as trivial as this?"

There is nothing in this world that is simple or trivial in our eyes. In my eyes, you are all my children. Whatever you ask of me, I will put out my greatest effort to attain on your behalf if it is in your best interest. And if it is not in your best interest, then I will still put out my greatest effort to bring you what is closest to that intention, that prayer, that wish that you have sent out to me, but also, in accordance with your highest interest and the highest and purest light.

Call upon me even when you are not certain that what you want is of light, and trust me that if it isn't, I will make sure that a light version of that be applied to your life, that a good version of that be offered to you, that a pure version of whatever you have asked for be given to you.

And I will do everything in my power to align my own prayers with yours and the prayers of all the ascended beings of light, all the cosmic beings of light, and the cosmic light itself, and to offer it before the throne of the Undifferentiated Source, before the throne of all the masters and mistresses, all the way from where I am to where you are and from where we both are to the great central Sun of this cosmic system of light where the United States holds its heart core.

The heart core of the Undifferentiated Source has opened up and asked that we all come back in oneness. While we have this opportunity, let us pray, pray, pray that we can all return to oneness.

Let us pray that we leave no one, no soul, even if it is as small as a pinhead, behind. No soul is unworthy. Whatever their size, whatever their destiny, whatever their service, whatever their desire, no soul is to be disregarded, ignored or discriminated upon. Every soul is to return to light. Every soul has been invited to return to the heart core of the Undifferentiated Source.

Pray with me, my children. Pray, pray, pray. Pray for yourselves. Pray for your loved ones. Pray for your enemies ten times more, a hundred times more.

Pray for all souls. Pray for all kingdoms. Pray for all manifested and un-manifested matter and non-matter. Pray, pray, pray.

And remember me in your prayers. I am your mother Mary. I love you and bless you and pray for you from the heart of love, from the heart of light, from my own heart.

I love you. I pray for you. I cherish you. I adore you.

Metatron

Metatron— whose name in Greek, *Meta-throno,* means *after the throne*— is the highest being of light in the hierarchy of light beings related to angels, ascended masters and cosmic beings of light. He is the guardian of light in manifest form. He is of the angelic realm. He has also lived in human form— as the prophet Enoch, who was the father of Methuselah and the seventh patriarch after Adam. The Bible says Enoch lived for 365 years. *Having walked with God, Enoch was seen no more because God had taken him away.* (Genesis 5:24)

Metatron is known to be *Yhwh* (Yahweh), a form of the Hebrew God used in the Old Testament. It means God in form or God of those made of form. "From the beginning of time and even before time ever existed," Metatron says, "I have served the physically created and manifest universe and beyond with light. I have spread my light, the light of Yahweh, upon all created, physically manifested forms."

In the ancient Hebrew mysteries known as the Kabbalah, Metatron is the guardian of the Tree of Life. He sits at the top of the tree in the first house known as Ketter (which corresponds to the crown chakra) and he sits at the very bottom, in the tenth house of the Tree of Life. In this tenth house, he is known as Sandalphon.

As Metatron has explained to me, in the beginning when there was only a great void and God was all there was, God said: Let there be light and let me become many. Then Archangel Metatron, at the command of God, brought the entire manifested form of all beings (including all the kingdoms— plants, animals, minerals, and so forth) into physical matter, spanning over universes, omniverses and beyond which, he says, we cannot possibly understand.

Then the spirit of God, like a breath, came over all that was manifested and brought it to life and action. That spirit of God is known as the I AM That I AM, God in action.

The terms I AM That I AM, I AM, I AM Presence, Magical Presence of the I AM, or the Spirit of the I AM all refer to the same spirit of God within us. This presence exists within us as the spark of God within our own hearts and it also exists in the heart core of all living things. It also exists as the supreme presence hovering above us, preparing us to receive it, embrace it and become it.

Once we become one with the spirit and embody the presence of the I AM, then we have fully attained mastery and achieved enlightenment. On the path of enlightenment, we find our own soul lineage of light and remember many past lives. In order to return to oneness, we need to remember all the events of all our incarnations that have brought us this far away from our I AM Presence.

At the turn of the new century, Metatron asked me to begin channeling what he called "life readings" for anyone who was drawn to find their life's mission by recalling their soul lineage of light, that is, their true origin.

For the most part, we do not consciously remember our past lifetimes but on a subconscious level, we do remember our origins. However, because of this difficult age in which we live and the increasing energetic density of our world, more and more of us are unable to connect to our origins even on a subconscious level. And when we forget, we feel lost, confused and disconnected in our lives.

Metatron created the framework for the life readings, which involve Spirit— that is, one or more of a person's guardians, an angel or an ascended master— speaking through me directly to the person receiving the reading. The kind of information given varies but Spirit always reminds us of our life's mission, our reason for being here now, the all-important purpose of our life. (See www.nasrinsafai.com/lifereadings for more about life readings.)

The Time Has Come for Great Changes

Metatron, channeled May 14, 2003

I offer you love, I offer you great love,
I offer you tough love. The choice is yours...
I love you so much that I am willing to give you
whatever it takes to make you see the path of light.

Beloveds of my own heart, I am Metatron. Take a deep breath with me and join me in spreading the light from the heart core of the Undifferentiated Source to the multitudes of souls in all levels and dimensions of realty.

From the beginning of time and even before time ever existed, I have served the physically created and manifest universe and beyond with light. I have spread my light, the light of Yahweh, upon all created, physically manifested forms.

The time has come for great changes in the direction that we are leading. The time has come for us to lead you back to light. To do this, we must ask you to clear and cleanse yourselves from all dross, all darkness and all negative emotions, to call upon all your guardians and guides to relieve you of all darkness and negativity.

The time has come to set the motion with faster pace in the direction of light on the journey homebound. God, the Undifferentiated Source, has requested your presence back to your source and we are about to speed up the process of folding these manifest universes upon themselves and unfolding themselves back in the heart of the Undifferentiated Source.

The Undifferentiated Source is God at that point of its existence where it has not separated itself from its own being-ness. God in its all-ness and in its is-ness is one large mass of wholeness and holiness. In that wholeness and holiness, no dross is allowed, no darkness can come in, no negativity will be allowed.

To bring you back, we must make sure that you become whole and that you become holy. To bring you back holiness, we have to bring back all the missing parts of your heart and your soul. To bring those missing parts, we have to heal you.

Healing your heart and your soul, reminding you that you are not alone will be the safest way and the fastest way to bring you back home.

But to do this, we must ask you to help us. We must ask you to seriously consider accelerating your own pace in the direction of spiritual evolution and walking the path of light.

That means letting go of many of your own self-interests in the human world of greed and personal wants, whims, wishes and desires, and to become focused on the light and the world of inner peace and harmony without the external dysfunctions.

This means clearing and cleansing your body, your mind, your emotions and your soul of all self-interest, self-centeredness, self-importance, of all victimization.

It means truly returning to the place of loving all, loving yourself, knowing yourself, knowing your own heart, knowing and remembering that the heart of God resides in your own heart, that the heartbeat of God beats to the same rhythm of your own heart and the heartbeat of Mother Earth, your mother planet, also pulses to your heartbeat as it pulses to the heartbeat of the Undifferentiated Source. She has now agreed to raise her own vibration. She has changed the rhythm and the pulse of her heartbeat.

This is why the changes in weather patterns, the changes in human patterns, the changes in life patterns are happening rapidly, unfolding before your eyes.

You must keep pace with the pace of Mother Earth. You must change the rhythm of your own heart to pulse with the heartbeats of Mother Earth, which is tuning itself, receiving an atonement, an at-oneness with the heart of the Undifferentiated Source.

When your heart beats in at-one-ment with the heart of Mother Earth, prosperity and abundance, peace and harmony will follow. When you choose to go it alone, you will find yourself lonely in this world and your world will become more fierce and your fears will increase because you will be left out of the main peace, the main rhythm.

Mother Earth is returning to its source in the heart of the Undifferentiated Source. She will do this with or without you. Why not join her? After all, does not a mother know what the child needs best? What do you have to lose from listening to her pleas?

She is no longer capable of supporting you. How can you be supported if you do not support her on her endeavor to attain more light and to return to God? How can she assist you and rescue you from pain and misery?

This is a two-way street. What you give to Mother Earth she can magnify a hundred fold, a thousand fold, ten thousand fold and return to you.

If you give it in goodness and righteousness, you will get it back in the same way. If you give it in greed, in fear, in victim-hood, in pain and in suffering, you will receive that back magnified and multiplied. The choice is yours.

As the highest being of light in the hierarchy of light beings, I, Metatron, offer my light to you.

***Take my offer and relieve yourself of all darkness.
Return to the heart of the Undifferentiated Source.
Return to love and light that are your
divine right, your divine heritage.***

Your Father-Mother God in Heaven has called you to join them back in Heaven. Drop your measly toys, your meaningless pastimes, your forgetful ways and run to the bosom of your Father-Mother God self.

Remember yourself as the self of God. Know that your divine rightful place is in the heart of the Undifferentiated Source.

The gates of Heaven have opened up to you. The palace of the heart of the Undifferentiated Source, the source of your Father-

Mother God, has opened its doors, receiving you in great glory. Come when you are called, not when the doors are closed.

I stand over you and all the ascended masters with great love, compassion and patience. I offer you love, I offer you great love, I offer you tough love. The choice is yours. I love you so much that I am willing to give you whatever it takes to make you see the path of light. And if that means tough love, so be it.

With great love, with great joy to have brought you this far, I stand at your feet as your father, as your humble servant, as your mother, as your friend, as love. I am Metatron.

First and Last Mantra

Commentary: We have given this mantra this title because Metatron says it is the 'be all and end all of mantras.'

You may recognize these words from the Bible (John 11:25). Jesus said them when he arrived at the home of Lazarus, who had died only four days before, and Lazarus' sister Martha told Jesus that if only he had come sooner, he could have saved her brother from dying. Jesus said to her: 'I am the resurrection and the life. He who believes in me will live, even though he dies; and whoever lives and believes in me will never die.' Then Jesus brought Lazarus back to life.

Recite this mantra often, as many times as possible during your waking hours. If you are in fear or other discomfort, the energies of these words will bring you peace and harmony.

Metatron, channeled August 10, 2003

Mantra

I AM the life and the resurrection.
I AM the resurrection and the life.

Beloveds of my own heart, I am Metatron. I could speak for three days and will not have covered all aspects of this mantra. The analogy is similar to that of the phoenix rising from the ashes. From life we have come, to life we will go, but before there was life, what was there?

The analogy of the ashes is to say that from the void we have come, and ultimately to the void we will go. Coming out of the void is a process of resurrection. It is a process of moving in the direction of light. It is a process of rising from the dead because in the void there is no individuality. The void is assimilated to death.

It is from rising from the dead that we come to life and it is from coming to light that we rise to our own individuality, our own consciousness, and understand that we have an identity—admitting or accepting, imbuing one's self with the understanding that I AM is the end all, be all of existence in its highest form. I AM in the void is moving to the surface and taking form.

Then saying *I AM the resurrection and the life* means the I AM from the center of the great void brought the resurrection of light. I AM rose in light and brought life to itself. *I AM the resurrection and the life.* I AM has risen and taken life. I AM has taken life and has resurrected.

So, it encapsulates all that comes from the nothingness, which is the void, into life, into existence, into expansion, into being-ness in all its forms, and then all of that is risen to light and ultimately given life.

Once that life has come to its fullest, it will return into its existence in the great void. [Where the Undifferentiated Source— that is, God in unmanifest form— resides holding the I AM within itself.]

So, I AM is the resurrection from the void. I AM is the life that the risen Christ, the risen soul, will take upon itself. When that life has ended, it is I AM that resurrects itself back from the void.

It is a complete cycle of rising and falling— rising, taking a life, ending a life, entering into the void and rising again. So, *I AM the resurrection and the life* takes you from the void to life. *I AM the life and the resurrection* takes you from life to the void to the resurrection again, to rise again. It becomes a complete cycle. You go into the void, rising from the void, taking a life, giving out that life, entering the void and rising again.

I AM the resurrection and the life calls to you all the energies of being-ness. It is as though you are encapsulating, and taking one capsule that contains within it all that is, everything that you can imagine in the created universe and everything that is in its non-manifest form in the void, everything that is in the light and everything that remains in the shadows.

All of creation and even all of that which remains uncreated is in that one sentence. It gives you the power of life. It gives you the power of non-life. It gives you the power of all that is in its manifest and non-manifest form.

It is a very powerful sentence. It is the be all and end all of all. It is the beginning and the end.

Meditation on the Blue Flame of Mercy

Commentary: The Blue Flame of Mercy resides in the heart core of God. This is a powerful meditation that carries energies of divine love to our individual hearts. It is helpful in cases of extreme trauma, such as experiencing the loss of a loved one or great destruction.

Metatron likens this exercise to 'a nectar to bathe the bodies, to shield, to cleanse from within and from without.' He gave this in response to a request from a group of light workers in New York and New Jersey who had been deeply traumatized by the twin towers disasters of September 11, 2001.

At each of the energetic focal points of the visualization— both at and between chakras— take a few deep breaths and repeat the mantra.

Metatron, channeled September 28, 2001

Visualization

• At the heart chakra

Envision a royal blue flame in your physical heart or heart chakra. The size of the flame is the circumference of the index finger and the thumb when they are joined at their tips.

• Between the fifth (the navel or solar plexus) and fourth (heart) chakras

From there, visualize this royal blue flame sitting inside your body two fingers below the rib cage. Feel the flame warm your body and begin to spin. As it spins, your stomach or solar plexus area begins to warm up. Sit with this image and take a few deep breaths.

• At the heart chakra again

Visualize slowly moving the flame up the body in the chest. Now the flame is spinning in the center of your chest and warming up that area as it spins.

- **At the thymus gland, between the heart and throat chakra**
Continue moving the blue Flame of Mercy up the body, spinning it through the thymus gland.

- **At the throat chakra**
Spin the blue flame up to your throat chakra.

- **At the third eye chakra**
Spin the blue flame up to your third eye chakra.

- **At the crown chakra**
Finally, spin the flame up until it reaches the crown on top of the head.

You will feel this internal flame warming up each of these areas, although the skin will remain cool. The blue flame will clear and cleanse all traumas from the body and restore your body, mind and soul to perfect healing and wholeness.

Mantra

I AM Light.
I AM Love.
I AM Bliss.

I AM Body Immortal.
I AM Life Eternal.
I AM Spirit Embodied.

I AM Light.
I AM Love.
I AM Bliss.

I AM Life Eternal.
I AM Body Immortal.
I Am Spirit Embodied.

I AM Light.
I AM Love.
I AM Bliss.

Mantras for God Unity

Commentary: To achieve God unity, to reverse our journey from duality, we must embody the I AM That I AM and become the image and presence of God in action. To achieve that, we must clear all obstacles on our path.

The following two mantras and invocation will help us on our path to God unity. Say the invocation first, then the Mantra for Clearing Obstacles and then the Mantra for Embodiment of the I AM That I AM. Metatron suggests we recite these daily in the format given and call upon a permanent spiral of the consuming flame of the violet fire to spin around our body. This spiral of violet fire will assist in removing pain and suffering, as well as karma.

Star Astrea, who is invoked here, is the feminine aspect of the Elohim of Purity. She is also called simply Astrea (Astra means stars in Greek). Invoking the presence of this great cosmic being will help to transmute the negativity around us. The Threads of Light that Metatron mentions are filaments of light that emanate from an awakened soul and connect to the mind of God.

Metatron, channeled October 9, 2002

Invocation

I call upon the guidance of Metatron and all the masters and mistresses of light to step forth to assist me in releasing my pain and suffering.

I call upon Elohim Star Astrea to cleanse and purify me.

I call upon the Violet Consuming Flame to clear me of all pain and suffering and karmic debts.

I call forth the ray of remembrance, the energies of empowerment and the light of clarity to come to my assistance.

I invoke the presence of the I AM That I AM to merge and unite with me. I immerse myself in its being-ness so deeply and so completely that I experience full merging now.

[Take a few deep breaths and pause for a moment; then follow with the next two mantras.]

Mantra for Clearing Obstacles

From the point of light where the Undifferentiated Source and I are one, I call upon the clearing and cleansing energies of the I AM THAT I AM.

From the point of light where the Undifferentiated Source and I are one, I call upon the Threads of Light to throw a blanket of protection over me and all that impacts me in my world.

I ask the I AM THAT I AM to manifest the electronic belt of protection around me and mine.

I ask the I AM THAT I AM to throw the magic circle of protection around me and mine.

I ask the magic circle of protection to cocoon me and mine.

I call forth Star Astrea to clear and cleanse my energy force fields of all that may intend harm.

I call forth the I AM THAT I AM of all the Ascended Masters, the Brotherhoods and Sisterhoods of Light to assist me with this intention.

With the presence of the I AM THAT I AM, I cleanse my path of all obstacles, all limitations, all shortcomings, all negative thought forms, and all cause and effect that may lead to harm.

I am the perfected mighty presence of the I AM THAT I AM.

The consuming flame of the mighty I AM THAT I AM will cleanse me and mine of all that is unlike itself, leaving me and mine in total purity and innocence.

I embody the perfection of the I AM THAT I AM everywhere I go in the inner and the outer realms.

I ask the I AM THAT I AM to manifest the electronic belt of protection around me and mine.

I ask the I AM THAT I AM to throw the magic circle of protection around me and mine.

I ask the magic circle of protection to cocoon me and mine.

I call forth Star Astrea to clear and cleanse my energy force field of all that may intend harm.

Mantra for Embodiment of the I AM That I AM

I AM the mighty power of perfected I AM THAT I AM.

The perfected I AM THAT I AM in me will make right all wrongs.

The perfected I AM THAT I AM in me will transmute all negativity.

The perfected I AM THAT I AM in me is all-knowing, all-seeing, all-acting in God's Truth.

I AM the embodiment of this Truth.

I AM the embodiment of God's Love.

I AM the embodiment of God's Light.

I AM the embodiment of God in Action.

I AM THAT I AM.

Light I AM.

Love I AM.

Bliss I AM.

Mantra for the Return of Shamballa (Heaven) on Earth

Commentary: This is a mantra to raise the energies of light for the return to Earth of Shamballa or Paradise and for the elevation of Mother Earth into her ascended state. It was given for the anchoring of Shamballa energies in the Gobi Desert in Mongolia on February 2, 2000. The date (2-2-2000) is significant. It was the first time in the new millennium when the month, the day and the year resonated with the number 2 and the energies of duality.

The prayer ceremony that was held in the Gobi began the process of releasing all of humankind from duality and returning us to unity, back in Shamballa, where, by our own divine right as light beings, we should once again reside.

This mantra still needs to be recited in order to elevate all souls to the higher levels of light. Every time we recite this mantra individually or collectively, we raise the vibration of light within ourselves and upon the Earth plane, which gets us closer to attaining Heaven on Earth.

Metatron, channeled May 5, 1999

Chant Om seven times.

Say: *Let the doors of Shamballa open to Earth and humanity in the name of the Twelve and the One.*

Chant Om seven times.

Say: *I AM the truth of the omnipotent essence of the Undifferentiated Source.*

I AM the peace of the omniscient essence of the Undifferentiated Source.

I AM the love of the omnipresent essence of the Undifferentiated Source.

I release all bonds, all ties, all contracts and all karmic connections from my omnipotent, omniscient and omni-present being now and forever.

I will all negative ties to be cut, severing bondage from any and all energies whose intention is to stop or delay the ascension process of Earth and all souls.

I am the power of the essence of the Undifferentiated Source.

I AM, I AM, I AM.

So it is. It is done.

Shamballa resides on Earth now and forever.

By the grace of the Undifferentiated Source, in the name of the I AM That I AM, and through the guardianship of the Seven Mighty Elohim, I ask that Shamballa remain intact, untampered with, unharmed and victorious from eternity to eternity.

Amen.

Mantra for Pure White Light

Commentary: This is a mantra for those times when you feel the need to clear and cleanse yourself of negativity, when you feel drained from being in crowded frenzied places— such as airports, train stations, shopping malls, traffic jams. This is meant to bring you to an extra peaceful state in a loving, nurturing space.

Metatron, channeled May 5, 1999

Pure Light I AM.

Point of Light I AM.

Light I AM.

I command the Light from the heart of Metatron to engulf me now.

I command the purity from the heart of Buddha to engulf me now.

I command the compassion from the heart of Quan Yin to engulf me now.

I command the Light from the heart of the Undifferentiated Source to engulf and protect my energy fields and keep me in bliss now and forever.

I command the Light from the heart of the Undifferentiated Source to instantaneously transmute all that I carry and absorb from people, places and things into pure white Light.

It is done. Amen.

Mantra for Money

Commentary: This mantra will serve us when we are ready to make serious and permanent changes to elevate ourselves from the pain and hardship of material lack. At the root of this prayer is the belief that we are truly worthy of abundance— yes, money. It is a prayer to empower us to believe this, to elevate our sense of self worth to the point where we know that we are worthy of having not just enough to pay our monthly bills but having more than enough— having abundance.

Say this morning and night and during the day whenever you find that your focus is falling away from peace and harmony.

Metatron, channeled September 3, 2002

I call upon the energies of the Undifferentiated Source to release me from all fear relating to money, all fear relating to wealth, and all fear relating to abundance.

I call upon the energies of the Undifferentiated Source to release me from the consciousness of lack.

I call upon the energies of the Undifferentiated Source to release me from the fear of surrender.

I surrender to pure white Light.

I surrender myself to the golden ray of transmutation.

I surrender myself to the platinum ray of manifestation.

I surrender myself to the silver ray of creation.

I surrender myself to the purple ray of transmutation.

I surrender myself to the green ray of hope.

I surrender myself to the golden white ray of faith.

I surrender myself to the maroon-magenta ray of compassion.

I surrender myself to the peach ray of clarity.

I surrender myself to the citron green ray of abundance.

I surrender myself to the aquamarine blue ray of peace and harmony.

I surrender myself to the Nile blue ray of power.

I surrender myself to the yellow ray of healing.

I surrender myself to the orange ray of passion to create.

I surrender myself to the red ray of creativity.

I surrender myself to the dark blue ray of mastery.

I surrender myself to the will of God.

I align my will with the will of God.

I free myself from the law of free will.

I will myself to live in bliss.

I will myself to live in divine love.

I will myself to live in the light of the Undifferentiated Source.

Light of God I AM.

Love of God I AM

Bliss of God I AM.

Will of God I AM.

I will it so.

So it is.

Amen.

Hallelujah!

Healings at Five Chakras: Throat, Heart, Solar Plexus Sacral Plexus and Root

In the following healings, Metatron focuses on five chakras to remove the emotional, mental and physical pain that we have incurred from this and other lifetimes. Each chakra is a disc-like concentration of energy that spins clockwise. *Chakra* is Sanskrit for wheel. The five chakras of Metatron's focus connect us to the earthly realms. Our two higher chakras, the third eye and the crown, are our connection to the heavenly realms.

Sometimes we are unconscious of how acute our pain is, and some of us either deny the pain or refuse, however unconsciously, to let the pain go. So, look deeply within yourself to know your truth. If you are ready and willing to let go of the pain and the scars that you have carried around for lifetimes, these healings can be instantaneous. If the healing is not immediate or even apparent, you will have, at the very least, embarked on a journey of recovery. In some cases, the pain is so severe, that it will take several and perhaps many repetitions of these healings, each working its way through the layers of scarring.

Metatron invokes many ascended and cosmic beings of light that you may not be familiar with. Their very presence, whether you consciously know of them or not, is sufficient for these healings to take place. Sometimes he invokes aspects of himself, as when he calls on Archangel Sandalphon, Archangel Metatron, and El Shadai.

When Metatron speaks of our "blueprint," he is referring to God's original plan for us as divine human beings. To achieve the seventh golden age and to attain mastery and move into ascension, we need to return to our original blueprint and remember that the spark of God is within us. All of these healings help to bring back the memories of that divinity and reestablish the original blueprint inside our body and being.

When you have finished each of these exercises, take a deep breath and remain still for as long as you need to be.

Healing of the Throat Chakra

Commentary: The throat chakra is the energetic center for communication. It sits directly behind our throat. In its natural healthy state, it vibrates a blue energy. When we have energy blockages, the color of the chakra turns dark and murky. This murky energy appears every time we cannot express our truth, communicate with others and speak of our needs and desires.

You may have noticed that sometimes during spiritual exercises or meditation, you or others begin to cough. Coughing can be a helpful way of pushing the pain and the obstacles that have accumulated in the throat chakra out of the body.

Now take a deep breath and invoke the presence of Metatron to begin the clearing of the throat chakra.

Metatron, channeled July 6, 2003

Beloveds of my own heart, I am Metatron. Take a deep breath with me. I want you to become aware of your body from the top of your head, going down all the way, chakra by chakra, and make the intention that if there are any other chakras needing attention, a clearing will be done. And we will work specifically with each issue as you see fit.

Let us go to the area of the throat. That chakra, when it is healthy and whole, should be a sphere, a disk of blue light, Nile blue, deep dark blue light, and it spins clockwise.

If it is not vibrating the blue light and there is a murky brown, the brown then needs to be removed. Behind the brown is the blue. Let us put in the intention for clearing, and ask Archangel Michael and Lady Quan Yin to come in and bring forth the energies of the purple and blue healing rays, and the energies of the Blue Sword of Fire.

Now let us ask that this chakra start spinning clockwise as it should.

[For a quick healing exercise that can easily be done throughout the day anywhere to clear the throat chakra, simply envision blue light surrounding the throat chakra as this wheel of energy spins clockwise.]

Healing of the Heart Chakra

Commentary: To bring healing and wholeness to the heart, we must address all issues of heartbreak and heartache from our birth to now and in other incarnations that have left scars, sometimes permanently over lifetimes. The longer the pain has persisted, the harder it is to remove and the more often the healing needs to take place. The heartache doesn't have to be of a romantic nature. It could be that your heartache is from the divorce of your parents when you were a child or the sickness or death of a loved one.

Behind every physical ailment is an emotional issue and, in the case of the heart, emotional issues manifest in all forms of physical heart problems, such as faulty heart valves, blocked blood vessels, and so on.

Metatron, channeled July 6, 2003

Beloveds of my own heart, I am Metatron. Let us go to the area of the heart.

Let us begin this process of healing of the grave issues of heartache that leave scars and affect the being in every aspect. Let us go to the root cause and eliminate the cause— the cause which has not been in agreement with original causes, the cause which has not been in agreement with the divine plan of God, the cause which is not in agreement with divine love, the universal law which humanity has separated itself from for so long, and which humanity is separating from even further at this present moment.

Although the impact of the healing process can be instantaneous, it usually takes time. Usually, in your normal world, such issues are dealt with in reverse order. In other words, you first notice the pain manifested in the physical body in the form of an ailment. Then if the person is lucky enough to know that there are emotions behind the physical ailment, they will look into the emotions. Finally, the person will move into the thought form and into changing the thought form, and ultimately into the root cause.

So, what you and I are doing right now is going directly to the root cause and removing and dissolving the pain that caused any incidents, the lessons that created the rift, the scar.

Then we are going to send the healing throughout the several body systems and ultimately, we will reestablish the original blueprint on top of the one that has been scarred. Over a period of time, the original blueprint will take over and the healing of the scars will take place.

When the root cause has been removed, imagine if the heartache had not happened in your life, how would you be looking at your world? Differently, correct? So then, let's go back to the heart. Let's go back to the root cause.

Let us command the universe to remove and dissolve the root cause. And we call upon Archangel Michael with his Sword of Blue Flame and his Cross of Blue Fire to remove the cause.

Whatever agreements, whatever contracts, and whatever karma of the past, karma of other lifetimes, has brought about the pain and the scars into this lifetime, the pain needs to be released and dissolved and removed from the conscience, subconscious and all deep levels of consciousness and knowing, deeper and deeper until the full completion, annihilation, removal.

And to complete this course, we call upon the consuming flame of the Violet Ray, the consuming flame of the Violet Ray, the consuming flame of the Violet Ray.

You may feel a spinning motion. You may feel nausea. You may feel as if your head is spinning. All of this is in order because you are spinning in time and space to that place in your karmic past where there is a root cause of any event that has left you scars. We go to where each incident was created. The consuming flame of the Violet Fire will clear all pain.

Now I will call upon the Cosmic Christ Heart Flame to replace that pain with the joy and the consciousness of the Christ. There will be a shift in your own essence, in your own body, in your own consciousness. Know that each of these scars is like a string, a thread that tugs at your heart, and it connects to many lifetimes.

If you give me permission, with the help of Archangel Michael and the beloved essence of our Lord Christ, and the cosmic levels of light, and the presence and the name of the I AM That I AM to clear the entire string of events, I will clear the entire lineage of pain and lessons, completely and fully removing all impact from all lifetimes and replacing the original blueprint of divine love. I thank you.

If you wish to receive my healing, say:

I give permission to Metatron and all light
to continue this healing.

I welcome our blessed Saint Michael the Archangel and his consort Lady Faith, the Sword of Blue Flame, the Cross of Blue Fire, to remove all strands, all strings, all threads that have tugged at this heart, past, present, and future, creating negativity and fear, heartache and heartbreak; and to remove it completely and fully, past, present, and future from all dimensions and all realities.

And I call forth the beloved cosmic Christ to bring the cosmic Christ fiery heart flame and to place that heart flame of the Christ consciousness at all levels through and into the cosmic level, and allow and establish the cosmic light of divine love in replacement through the essence of the divine original blueprint as God intended.

Now that you have granted permission, say the following:

For the soul lineage of this physical embodiment and all physical embodiments of (say your name), I ask Metatron to now fill my heart with the light of the cosmic blueprint and to bring the light throughout my body.

I am still within this light. I make this light my own. I become this light and I know that I am pure light.

Now take a deep breath and imagine a shower of golden white light flowing from the top of your head to the tip of your toes, from the tip of your toes to the top of your head. Feel the tingling all over your body.

Take three deep breaths and repeat the visualization of the shower of golden light two more times.

Healing of the Solar Plexus Chakra

Commentary: In its perfect state, the solar plexus vibrates a golden yellow-orange color. When it does not, it vibrates murky colors. Those are the times when we feel stuck and we cannot move, basically when we are dis-empowered. Such situations instigate fear in us, fear of moving forward in life, fear of leaving abusive situations, fear of daring to want better for our life, fear even of change when it may be positive.

In this healing exercise, Metatron places in our energy field an etheric or energetic lotus to protect us from shutting ourselves out from light. Be aware that once you have received this, you must maintain it (by repeating this exercise) in order to continue receiving the light and be empowered.

If you feel stuck again after this exercise, please go back and redo the healing. It could be that you need to do it often at least for a while and also in times when you are in difficult situations that require you to empower yourself and take a leap of faith.

Metatron, channeled July 6, 2003

Beloveds of my own heart, I am Metatron. Let us move down and look at the energies of your solar plexus. Are you willing and ready to let go of these emotions that are not serving you for the highest light?

If you are willing, say:

Yes, I am willing to receive this healing.

Focus your intention on the solar plexus. I will call upon the energies and the forces of Archangel Uriel, the holder of inner light, the guardian of the soul, because the soul resides inside the solar plexus, and when events of negative nature impact the essence of the human being, it is the soul that is pushed into the recesses. And it is the soul that cannot complete its mission of light because of the pain and the suffering and because of the lack of empowerment, the disempowerment that takes place as a result of such events.

Once we remove the negativity from the event, we can remove the disempowerment. Then the essence of your being will be ready and prepared to take on issues of power and victory, conquering, and success that will manifest not only in the spiritual arena but in the mundane level of existence.

So, take a deep breath. Again, I ask your permission to perform this healing. If you are ready and willing, say that you are.

I call upon the assistance of Archangel Uriel in both male and female aspects, Archangel Sandalphon in both male and female aspects, and Archangel Michael and Lady Faith.

Focus your attention on the solar plexus and know that the murky colors are being released. Even more importantly, a very large yellow colored lotus is now in place facing your belly button.

The lotus is positioned behind your navel. It is positioned as though it is swimming in water; the petals are facing outward toward your belly and the core of it is sitting right behind your belly button. It is emanating a golden yellow light outward through your belly button.

The emanations of light pouring out from the lotus create an egg shaped oval outside of your body, protruding about a foot in front of your belly button and another foot into your belly button into the back of your body at mid-spine across the spinal column.

I will begin to spin this light, calling for assistance from Archangel Uriel, Archangel Sandalphon, Archangel Metatron, Archangel Michael and Lady Faith, the Cosmic Christ, the Fiery Light, the Blue Cross of Fire, The Blue Sword of Mercy, the White Blazing Fire of Light, The Blue Ray of Will, the Green Ray of Truth, the Pink Ray of Divine Love, the Ruby Red Ray of Universal Brotherhood and Sisterhood of Service, the Violet Consuming Ray, and I ask that the root cause of all pain and suffering be removed.

I call upon Maha Chohan; Lord Lanto, the holder of the Ray of Divine Wisdom; and Master Paul; and El Morya and Archangel Michael, the holders of the Ray of Divine Will to replace all the negativity from this incarnation all the way through all incarnations to the original blueprint of the I AM That I AM, the soul signature of [say your name].

Take a deep breath and pause for a moment to receive the blueprint.

Repeat the following three times:

I am fully and completely established in the white light.
I am restored to health and wholeness.

I now command, in the name of the I AM That I AM, that the original blueprint of the magical mighty presence of the I AM That I AM for the soul presence be reestablished in the body, mind, emotions, and spirit of the essence of this being who has taken human embodiment and chosen the name [say your name].

Healing of the Sacral Plexus and Root Chakras

Commentary: The sacral plexus and root chakras are almost always in need of attention to be restored to health and wholeness. The reason for this is that we are now living in an age where abuse to our own bodies and the body of our planet, our Mother Earth, is rampant. What we do to our planet is felt in our bodies, especially in the last two chakras because these two are our connection to Earth.

The sacral plexus includes our procreative organs and connects us to our spiritual creativity, as well as our physical creative forces. When these energies are blocked, we may experience depression and, if severe enough, the lack of will to live because they impact our solar plexus, which is our will center.

The root chakra is our connection to Mother Earth and our spirit's connection to our physical body. Due to the hardship that we experience in this world of chaos, many of us, especially the very old souls among us, are tired of living here on Earth and this has created root chakra problems, which show up in such manifestations as lower back pains, sciatica, hip problems and imbalances on the right and left side of the body.

Clearing these chakras will not only help to get rid of the pain but will also help us become more hopeful and have new zest for life.

Metatron, channeled July 6, 2003

Beloveds of my own heart, I am Metatron. Let us take our attention down to the two last chakras, the sacral plexus and root chakra. We will perform this healing on both of these chakras for they are both connected and for the most part, they hold the same energies.

In certain members of your species, the root chakra would be connected to rooting and grounding and feeling that you belong. The sacral plexus relates to relationships, intimacy.

In those of you who are more highly evolved, the two become one because the issue of intimacy and communion in physical love in itself will not have meaning unless it has a connection with your relationship with others, and with your connection with the

Earth and the masses. It is when the species has not awakened or is of lower vibration that the two will need to be treated separately.

If you wish to receive this healing, say:

I [your name] wish to receive healing in my sacral plexus and root chakra, relieving me of all the pain and trauma caused in this and all other lifetimes.

I will call upon the energies of Archangel Sandalphon; the energies of Archangel Gabriel the Messenger, the one that has always remained by your side reminding you that you are a messenger yourself and that your message is one of purity and peace, one of divine love, one of harmony and unity. Archangel Gabriel is a very good friend, a very close friend. Use Gabriel's wisdom and love, and remember to call upon Gabriel frequently.

I call upon Archangel Metatron; Lord Lanto the guardian of wisdom; Lord El Morya the guardian of will power; Lord Paul the Venetian, the guardian of divine love; Lady Nada, the guardian of brotherhood and sisterhood of service; and Lady Quan Yin, the guardian of compassion and mercy.

I call upon Lord Hilarion the guardian of truth; Lord Michael, in this case as the guardian of victory and beauty; Archangel Uriel, the guardian of inner light; Archangel Metatron, the guardian of outer light; and Metatron as El Shadai, the glory of the Throne of Grace; and Metatron as Metathrono, the Throne of Grace.

And we follow the threads to the root cause— the root cause being your presence here on Earth— in order to remember that your home is in the heart of God and that the only way out of this darkness is by turning around and making the journey returning to the heart of God.

The purpose of this exercise for you is to remove all the pain you have experienced in the past, present and future in this lifetime and in all lifetimes, and to establish this truth on behalf of the masses and on behalf of Mother Earth, and to remove the troubles, and the turmoil, and the trauma that you have experienced, and the loneliness that you have felt throughout many life times.

Healing colors are now illuminated in the lower regions of your body. These colors range from electric blue light to emerald green to rose pink to deep blue to pure white light to golden yellow to the pearlescent opalescent illumined light of God Unity.

May you be rooted in the knowing and the essence of God unity. May the entire lineage of light come to your rescue and to your assistance.

Sphere of Illumination

Commentary: The Sphere of Illumination— or as Archangel Michael calls it, the Sphere of Remembrance— holds within it the lineage of light from whence we have come. Our soul lineage includes all the drops from the ocean that we are. The Sphere of Illumination connects us to our soul lineage, brings back the memories of who we are and what our mission is on Earth. It also connects us with other soul members in our own lineage of light.

When you do this exercise at night, you go into the original essence of your soul lineage and benefit from receiving nurturance from highly evolved beings of your light family tree, including ascended masters and angelic beings. When you do this exercise during the day, you will come across other members of your soul tree who are in incarnation now and this will help you to recognize them.

Metatron places this sphere in the space of the cosmic heart, which is the area right over your thymus gland, located between your throat and heart chakra.

When you finish this exercise, take a deep breath and be still for as long as you need to be.

Metatron, channeled July 6, 2003

Beloveds of my own heart, I am Metatron. Take a deep breath with me. Envision in the center of your heart a blue flame, two inches high and an inch and a half wide. In the very center of this flame, you see pure white light. Around the white light, you see a golden halo. At the edge of the golden halo, you see blue flames, a blue burning flame of light. This is the flame of God Unity.

I will place a maroon colored sphere in your cosmic heart. The sphere is deep purple, maroon, and magenta. It is translucent. It is the size that if you were to cup both your hands and place them together, it would fit inside your cupped hands. This is the size of the sphere that sits in the center of your cosmic heart.

Now I will fill from the edge of the blue of the flame all the way to the edge of the sphere with a translucent transparent deep purple blue color. And as I fill it, it expands and you will feel the presence of this sphere within you inside your heart.

I place this sphere to invoke the healing and wholeness within you. This sphere begins to spin and colors begin to emanate from it. It begins with a very light pink, a rose pink, illuminating from the sphere, and this is to bring you the nurturance and the divine love from the heart.

The color then becomes deeper, turning a deep rose pink. As the sphere spins, beams of light emanate in every which direction into your body and your auric field.

This color of pink expands and illuminates, cocooning your auric field within itself, bringing the edges of your aura closer and yet making the entire cocoon more empowered and illumined.

Energetically, you will feel differently after this session. What you will feel is as though you have a layer of protection that helps you distinguish energy that's coming at you and assisting the process of you not absorbing all the ranges of energies but only of serving the higher light.

For the next few months, it will be beneficial for you if you could take a minute or two every day upon awakening to check upon this cocoon of light and to expand your Sphere of Illumination with this deep rose pink color, just to make sure that you have the area completely covered. Do the same at night. Changes and improvements will occur with each repetition of this exercise.

This exercise will also teach you how you can heal yourself. The more you can cocoon yourself in the deep pink light, the more you can protect yourself.

Now, I am going to spin the sphere faster and faster. As I do, the color turns into pure white light. It may be a jolting feeling in that moment when you reach to 100 percent pure white light.

To complete this exercise, I will repeat to you the process. Twice a day, first thing in the morning upon arising and last thing at night before you fall asleep, focus your intention on the Flame of God Unity inside the Sphere of Illumination. The core of the flame is pure white light. Around the edge is a golden halo. Around the golden halo is a pure blue light. From the edge of the blue light to the edge of the sphere that sits around the flame there is a purple magenta transparent translucent sphere of light that creates the Sphere of Illumination.

This sphere is spinning at all times. When you wish to examine it, you can ask it to slow down and then you will see all of the colors all the way from the core of the flame all the way to the edge of this sphere.

As this sphere begins to spin, you will see ranges of color. It comes to rest as a very light rose pink. When this sphere spins, it becomes a deep rose pink. Deeper and deeper and deeper, as the spin becomes faster and faster and faster, to the point where you see nothing but a jolting pure white light that takes over the entire body, pulling in the auric field, cocooning it [the auric field] within itself [the expanded sphere], removing all cobwebs, all darkness, all gray matter and filling you with a pure white light.

At that point, if you are beginning your new day, offer your day to the pure light of the I AM That I AM and say:

I offer my day to the light of the I AM That I AM.

And if you are beginning your dream journey [that is, going to sleep], offer your dream journey to the pure light of the I AM That I AM and say:

I offer my dream journey to the light of the I AM That I AM. With the guardianship of Archangel Michael, I desire to go to the highest and purest realm of light where the greatest of teachings can be given to me.

At this point, if you so wish it, you can call upon me, Metatron, and I will be by your side.

Hecate

Much of what has been written about Hecate is confusing and contradictory. But perhaps there is reason for this. Hecate is a divinity of duality and transitions. She has been associated with both the dead and with newborns, with death and fertility. She has been depicted as young and beautiful and as an old hag.

In early Greek depictions, Hecate is a young maiden. Hecate stood guard at the Acropolis in Athens. But she also stood guard at the gateway to Hades. Later mythology gives her three heads: the head of a dog, a snake and a horse. She was also identified with the new dark Moon. And for some, she was the goddess of witchcraft and sorcery. By the Medieval ages, she was an evil crone. In his play Macbeth, Shakespeare makes Hecate the head witch in his bevy of witches whose words seem like a parody today— "Double, double, toil and trouble, Fire burn and cauldron bubble."

My first encounter with Goddess Hecate was when I saw her in a vision as an extremely beautiful and very sensuous woman, with long dark hair, wearing a red dress. When I first channeled Hecate, the room I was in filled with red light.

Several Wiccans who were among my students at the time were quite surprised to hear me describe Hecate as a stunning seductive woman. I didn't realize then that some Wiccans worshipped Hecate and they considered her to be a crone.

It makes sense that Hecate's choice of red is her signature energy because red is the color of Earth energy, sexuality (the lower chakras), and blood, the life substance that runs through our veins. She is here to cleanse the Earth of what does not belong here— the dross and negativity, the darkness.

I have also come to understand that Hecate, like Quan Yin, wields the enormous power of feminine love.

But who really is Hecate? I will let her tell you in her own words in the following transcription, The Queen of Hell.

The Queen of Hell

Commentary: The following was channeled in Puttaparthi, India on the day of the Festival of Lights (Diwali) in honor of Lakshmi, the Hindu goddess of spiritual and material abundance.

Hecate, channeled October 28, 1997

Who on Earth or Heaven would wish to be responsible for Hell and the Underworld? Hell is hell, and the Underworld is where souls for whom there is no hope are sent.

I am Hecate. My presence on this very special occasion has been requested. Special qualities rule the world of duality, and truly, it is very appropriate for me to be invited, for we still live in this world of duality.

[Our] purpose ... is to return to unity. I will be quite relieved when unity does happen, for I can then retire. There is a special retirement dimension that has been created especially for beings such as myself. Upon entering this dimension, there is a sign stating: "Entry Permissible for Retired Gods and Goddesses Only!"

But jokes aside, it may benefit you to receive a discourse on my purpose for existence and the nature of duality as I see it.

The purpose for my existence is to control duality, to put a leash on duality, and to awaken all beings from the slumber of forgetfulness and open their eyes to the truth of their unity.

In Greek mythology, Poseidon ruled the seas, Zeus was the father of all, and Athena was the warrior goddess. I, Hecate, am the Queen of Hell and the Underworld.

Sometimes when no one wants to accept the job that gives little pay and even less satisfaction, it gets passed around and around until someone shrugs their shoulders and says they will do the job, if only to get it out of the way. This is what I did.

Who on Earth or Heaven would wish to be responsible for Hell and the Underworld? Hell is hell, and the Underworld is where souls for whom there is no hope are sent. It is there that Hecate beats them up, puts a leash around their necks, and puts them to work until such time that they cleanse their karma and learn humility. After they have achieved a certain criteria, they can move out from Hell and the Underworld.

The purpose of God unity is to enfold Hell and the Underworld into light, to release it and to return it to the heart of God, to the heart of the Source.

In the beginning of our acquaintance, this channel (Nasrin Safai) had great reservations about working with me or even allowing me to be around. Just like many others, she had a certain degree of fear, which made her not want anything to do with me.

At that time, she was deeply involved with working with Quan Yin, and she was deeply involved with praying to be aligned with the will of God, as she still is. There are many layers of alignment with the will of God, and as your prayers are answered, you move from one layer to the next, all the while continuing your prayers for alignment.

The channel cleared the room and called upon the Throne of Grace, requesting Quan Yin. Her request was granted and Quan Yin appeared to her.

After conversing with Quan Yin in her inner realm, Quan Yin turned her back to the channel and rather than the back of Quan Yin, there was the face and body of Hecate.

Whereas Quan Yin was wearing white, Hecate was wearing dark red; and whereas Quan Yin had an innocent, loving face, Hecate had a sensual, feminine face.

***Quan Yin is the epitome of compassion;
Hecate is the epitome of power.***

The channel realized that Quan Yin and Hecate work closely together. In fact, they work back to back.

After having worked with both Hecate and Quan Yin for a few years, the channel introduced Hecate to a woman who has healed and served for over 40 years in your realm and is a great being of light.

The channel transmitted the energy of Hecate, and the woman, who was encountering Hecate for the first time, witnessed the room becoming filled with a powerful red energy, which hovered over the channel's head and then descended slowly into the channel as she began the transmission of Hecate's messages.

During the transmission, the woman saw a sensual, seductive young female dressed in red robes and wearing fine jewelry.

After the session, the woman was very affected by her experience with Hecate and said, "I have been waiting all my life to meet a guide like this who is so serious and powerful. I like working with her. I like this woman very much." And she thanked the channel for bringing the energy and healing of Hecate into her house.

The woman then asked the channel what she could do to honor Hecate, and the channel told her that Hecate likes the color red. So, she put on her ruby earrings and her ruby ring, which she had for over 30 years, but wore them only on special occasions. And she wore a red scarf and bought red candles to honor Hecate.

At the end of the channel's visit with her friend, I was a million times more impressed with this lovely woman than she was with me.

Just before the channel left the woman's house to return to her own home, I requested a few final words with our friend. I sat at her feet and I thanked her for her unconditional love and lack of judgment.

I allowed the channel to touch my heart and experience the pain of one who wields great power and is feared for her ruthlessness. And the channel cried for the pain that is part of Hecate.

You can understand the pain parents go through when their children are unruly and disobedient. I am as such a parent. I work with the unwilling, the unruly and the un-accepting. When light beings such as the channel and her friend have compassion and understanding for the wisdom that lies behind the power of Hecate, I show you my love with joy and humility.

I will tell you one last story before I leave you with my blessings. The channel was involved in a business transaction to purchase some small velvet pouches to give as gifts to people with crystals inside them. She was originally going to order the pouches to be made out of blue material to honor Lord Michael.

The shopkeeper went away and returned with a few yards of a dark red velvet. Immediately the channel thought of Goddess Hecate and as a way of honoring her, purchased the red pouches instead of the other color she was going to order.

When she later opened her package to inspect her purchases, she saw that in the bag were blue pouches as well as red, even though she had not asked for both.

Even Goddess Hecate honors Lord Michael and his legions and wished to invoke his blessings by including the blue pouches with the red.

Later that same day, the channel repeatedly offered prayers on behalf of Goddess Hecate. She gave thanks to God for Hecate's presence in her life and asked that her prayers for Hecate be accepted.

After enough times, her request was answered and her prayers answered.

My heart once again melted with humility to experience that kind of love for one like me expressed in an Earthly being.

With great love and blessing, I honor all of you who read these words.

I am Hecate, the Queen of Hell and the Underworld.

And so it is.

Run to the Light

Hecate, channeled May 14, 2003

While I hold the leash upon the darkness, walk into the light. While you have the opportunity to gain headway, run in the direction of the light.

My beloved children, I am Hecate. As the Queen of Hell and the Underworld, I offer you my words of wisdom, my words of caution. The time has come when recognition of light and dark is becoming dimmer and you need to play your cards very smartly to know who is truly offering you light and who isn't.

I hold the leash and the reign upon the forces of darkness. Their purpose for existence is to guide you to light even though it may not seem that way. They guide you in the direction of light by distracting you from it because they believe that if you had gained the worthiness to be directed in the light, you would not be distracted from it.

Therefore, for as long as they can distract you, they will just show you that you have to earn the merits to become worthy of gaining the light. And you have to be vigilant and disciplined in calling forth the light, in blazing forth the light, in following the light, in becoming the light, in knowing the light.

Knowing the light is more than half the battle. Once you know what is light, then you know what is right. Once you know what is right, you would follow it. You wouldn't feed your children poisonous weeds because it is not right, because it will not bring them righteousness, because it will not give them sustenance. In the same way, you would not want your children to be astray, to run amuck and be distracted from the light. You would want your children to be given the opportunity to head in the direction of the light.

So, awaken to the light that is your divine right.

Take advantage of the guidance that is provided to you through the masters of light, mistresses of light, gods of light, goddesses of light, ascended beings of light, cosmic beings of light and cosmic light. Cosmic light is shining upon the four corners of this universe.

Those corners that are greatly hidden from the light are accumulating the dark and sinister forces. The dark forces run away from the light. Keep yourself in the light. That will be the fastest and the smartest way to return to peace and harmony. If you hide from the light, you will be mixing with the wrong crowds. If you move into the light, those crowds cannot follow you unless they drop their darkness too.

Be the role models, be the guiding light, be the pioneers, be the pinpoints of light, be the spearheads, be the beacons, be the light bearers, be the way-show-ers, be the light.

While I hold the leash upon the darkness, walk into the light. While you have the opportunity to gain headway, run in the direction of the light.

Become the light that is your divine right.

Become the light that brings you back safe and sound and know that I will do everything in my power to continue to hold the leash on the darkness.

I will do everything in my power to distract the sinister forces from following you.

Know that my prayers are there for you in the light.

Call upon me, your mother Goddess Hecate, to provide a shield of light around your bodies, to make you invisible to all the dark and sinister forces.

Call upon me, your mother Goddess Hecate, to distract the dark forces from your path.

Call upon me, your mother Goddess Hecate to remove, to annihilate, to destroy the dark and sinister forces that might create obstacles on your path of light.

And pray for me, your mother Goddess Hecate, that I may succeed always and forever in holding you in the light of God, the

Undifferentiated Source, the I Am That I Am, the self of all selves, your own true self, the source of all sources, the one and the only.

In your love, with great joy in offering you a great service, I Am That I Am. I am your mother Hecate.

So it is.

Oh, people of the world!
Verily, there hath come to you
a convincing proof from your Lord
For we have sent unto you
a light that is manifest.

- Qur'an, 4:174

Hilarion

The Ascended Master Hilarion is the Chohan of the Fifth Ray, which is the emerald green ray. When Hilarion first came to me, I did not know about the Seven Rays, so I could not have known that he was master of the Fifth Ray of Truth. When I first saw him, the entire room filled with green energy. I saw him in green robes and with a green jewel on a crown over his forehead. He spoke extensively about truth, about not wavering from our truth, because truth is God and truth doesn't need to be proved or defended.

Soon after this first communication with Hilarion, I happened to be in a bookstore and a book happened to fall, literally, off a shelf down at my feet. In this book— *The Mahatma* by Brian Grattan— I first learned about the Seven Rays, light emanations of the universal Christ consciousness, and their patrons or masters or chohans. (Another book that discusses the Seven Rays is *Lords of the Seven Rays* by Mark and Elizabeth Clare Prophet.) Later, I began to receive visions and there would be more channelings about the Seven Rays and their chohans.

The Seven Rays all stem from the pure white light ray. When light first came out of the void emanating from the heart core of the Undifferentiated Source, it was pure bright white light. This light then went through a prism, separating itself from its oneness into the seven colors of the rainbow. Each of the colors became one of the Seven Rays and an ascended being of light became the guardian of each ray.

Hilarion is said to have been Saul of Tarsus, who later became the apostle Paul. He is said to have reincarnated in the fourth century as Saint Hilarion, who was renown as a healer.

I have noticed that these masters of the Seven Rays work with me in seven-year cycles. Seven years ago, these masters began to lead me to a new level of awareness and understanding, and then they seemed to fade into the background, allowing me to experience life and gain from it, learning and growing consciously as a human in the modern world and as a spirited being growing at soul level.

Now, seven years later, they have begun to return with the same intensity as before. As Hecate says, there are many layers of alignment with the will of God, and as our prayers are answered, we move from one layer to the next, all the while continuing our prayers for alignment.

As Hilarion comes again with the energies of truth and the hope that truth shall be known, he raises my energy to that next level, the level I strive for, and when he feels I am at that level, he will no doubt retreat again into the background until I have gathered the necessary wisdom and I'm ready to go to the next level.

Journey to the Abode of Truth

Commentary: In this discourse, Hilarion takes us to the Abode of Truth. Prepare yourself as you would for meditation. Breathe deeply and find your stillness. As you go on this journey, you may see what Hilarion describes or you may feel sensations of coolness or heat or pressure or tingling in your body. You may see only colors. Or you may experience none of these. At a subconscious level, however, you have been touched by the energies imbued in this communion because Hilarion's words are imbued with the energies of the Abode of Truth. Simply by reading them, you come into these energies— how much depends on how open you are to receiving them.

The Threads of Light Hilarion speaks of are filaments of light that emanate from an awakened soul and connect to the mind of God.

Hilarion, channeled July 30, 2002

There are times when silence is the greatest solution. When your truth cannot be heard, silence is the answer.

Dearly beloveds, I am Hilarion. Feel the energies. I bring you an energy field of emerald green color. I bring to you the energies of the Ray of Truth.

Be vigilant from this day on with the words that you speak because these words will manifest. Be vigilant that your words are spoken in truth. Not even in facetiousness consider speaking untruths. Not even as a joke speak any untruths. As of this point, together we make a commitment to speak the truth and to vigilantly watch the mind. Think truthful thoughts.

I come to bring you strength to work with the Ray of Truth. Feel the energy field that I vibrate.

Envision yourself standing in front of me. Place the palm of your right hand in the palm of my right hand. We create together a force field of energies. I transfer to you the power to be in truth at all times.

I would like to take you on a journey. I would like to invite you to visit with me the Abode of Truth. Once you enter, you take a vow to stand in truth, and you will be imbued with the highest vibration of the Ray of Truth. You will feel the force field as an emerald green energy. Call upon the Threads of Light. Envision taking the end of a Thread and come with me to the Abode of Truth.

As you stand behind the golden door, knock and take a solemn vow that truthfulness will be the path that you tread upon from this moment on. And if you fear that you might not fully succeed, call upon the energies of Hilarion and ask that all which no longer serves you be released from you at the threshold of the Abode of Truth.

When you find yourself committed, the door will open to you. Enter and find the ascended master who will assist you in the process of purifying your being to hold the highest energetic vibration of the truth. Enter and receive.

You are now guided to stand under the ray through the pillar of light.

See in the center of this room a platform. As you move to stand in the center of the platform, a shower of light in the emerald green color opens up to you.

Absorb, receive and assimilate the Ray of Truth. Become one with it and intend to vigilantly stand in truth, the absolute truth. Ask that you would know the difference between truth and untruth.

If you are faced with untruth in others, you are not responsible to change them. You are responsible to maintain your own position in truth.

Watch as you merge with the emerald green ray. What parts of your body may show resistance in receiving this energy? Ask that the resistance be released.

As you step away from the platform, you are offered your ceremonial robes, your staff, your crown, and your cape.

Through the absorption of the Ray of Truth and the recalibration of your energy field, you have entered to yet another level of mastery. Whether you graduate this school of mastery or not depends on your conduct from now on.

You are responsible to act as a master would. You are responsible to speak with the great power of the truth and to stand by the absolute. You are not responsible to change others to see through your eyes or to understand your position.

When you are faced with challenging situations, you have a choice to take silence, to walk away, or to speak up.

There are times when silence is the greatest solution. When your truth cannot be heard, silence is the answer. Only when you can be certain that the truth will be heard, will make changes for positive reform, speak. Otherwise, silence.

A true master can differentiate between the time to speak up, the time to be silent, and the time to walk away. Standing in your truth does not have to make you unkind. In principle, you cannot compromise; nor can you jeopardize the absolute.

Truth does not defend itself. Therefore, it does not need to be offensive; nor does it need to be pushed upon anyone.

When the vibration of the light of truth is lacking, that is a signal to walk away. When you find a measure of light and a degree of acceptance, then you may speak. Speak the truth when you know it will be heard.

When it will not be heard, take silence. When you may jeopardize yourself or others, then the only choice left is to walk away. If you are pushed in compromising situations, you must take silence.

Understand that you are responsible to survive and to maintain this body, which is the Temple of God, in its wholeness. Therefore, if the price for speaking your truth is to lose your life, be silent.

When you are totally absorbed in the truth absolute, you have no need of defending yourself. That assists you in never moving to take offensive measures. If you are rejected, walk away.

Truth absolute is as God is. God never defends itself in its being-ness. God never takes offensive measures to prove its being-ness. The truth absolute is God.

When you fully absorb and understand the meaning of these words, you have graduated from the school of mastery. You will then hold so much power that you will not need to resort to defensive or offensive measures. The power of truth absolute will reign. You will become complete. Only then will you have absorbed and become one with the essence of truth absolute.

In pursuit of finding the self, humankind resorts to great complexities in life. As such, one loses the self in the complexity and the mind takes over, creating many dramas that take one further away from the simplicity of the self.

The truth is held within the realm of the simple self. When the complex processes are done and the return to simplicity is known again, humanity will find the true self and through that, the truth.

The truth is.

And so it is. I am Hilarion.

Comments on Hilarion from Metatron

Channeled July 30, 2002

Beloveds of my own heart, read and practice the words of Master Hilarion. You will find many levels of truth hidden in the simplicity of the words that he speaks. Only when you can see that truth will you become it.

Therefore, practice. Read the above words. Put them to good use. Every time you read these words, you will gain another insight into his teachings.

When we speak of truth absolute, that is the version of truth that doesn't need to be tampered with or does not have to match other people's mind frame or life style.

A lot of times you take the truth and you represent it from the angle you feel it will be accepted, whether it is about what is going on inside of you, within your own mind or in relation to another.

A simple example is a phone conversation. You may have a conversation with someone who always sees the positive in life. When you have your conversation with that person, normally you would not speak of your aches and pains. Your focus moves to the positive.

Within minutes, you may have another telephone conversation with a friend whose focus is the aches and pains, the agonies and tragedies of life. Immediately you change your energy field to match that person's field and you bring up those aspects of your day that match the negative impact of that day, your aches and pains, the negative events, the obstacles, the tragedies.

In that moment, what would serve you is to stand back and reexamine where is the line that you can draw to create a circle that you can call truth absolute. Are you having a great day today or are you having a difficult day today? You may say it never is black or white, and you are right; it isn't.

Therefore, is it necessary for you to go to the extreme of black for one minute and to the extreme of white the next minute? Is it necessary for you to create a drama of goodness in one conversation and the drama of obstacles in the next?

Is it important that you allow yourself to have a roller coaster ride according to your social or personal encounters? Is it necessary that when a co-worker approaches you with a problem, you immerse yourself in that problem? Or is it better that you stand in your truth? Are you in a greater position to help them if you merge in their drama or are you better equipped to assist if you stand in a neutral place?

In the same way, if someone approaches you with great joyful news, is it necessary for you to jump up and down to express joy on their behalf? Or is it more appropriate for you to remain neutral?

You understand this very clearly in a job setting. Apply that in all situations and you will see that there is a certain composure that you acquire in certain settings. Then you let that composure go because you feel those are walls.

The truth is, the walls are the dramas that you create as you try to please everyone because every drama that you create then manifests in your life. So, do not be surprised when after a conversation revolving around all aches and pains, you truly feel the aches and pains upon completing the conversation.

Inasmuch as you may go to one end of the spectrum, you can go to the other.

Either end of the spectrum is hard work. Staying in the center is easy.

Quan Yin

Quan Yin is the Goddess of Compassion and Mercy, and the Guardian of Mothers and Children. She is the female aspect of Buddha. She wears the image of Buddha as a headdress on her crown chakra. Legend has it that she was created from the tears of Buddha.

Quan Yin has also lived on Earth in human form. In one of her lifetimes here, she was the Buddhist saint Miao Shan, a healer known for her miracles. The purpose of that lifetime, Quan Yin says, was to anchor the energies of light, compassion, strength, divine power, and clarity of focus and intent.

"In every age I come to Earth," Quan Yin says. "I take on human form. It does not take away from the truth of my essence and my being-ness. It only adds to the truth of my essence that I would take human form. I need to feel the pain of being human so that I can have compassion for Earthly beings."

Quan Yin has been revered as a saint in the Orient for centuries. "In the Orient I am the embodiment of what the Blessed Virgin Mary represents in the West," Quan Yin says. "Mother Mary and Mother Quan Yin are one. We are the same. We are two drops from the same ocean."

"The Blessed Mother and I not only have very similar energies, but we have also chosen very similar tasks," she says. "We are both devoted to the children of the Earth. We are both devoted to the mothers of the Earth. We are both devoted to our duties as the feminine aspect of the Earth and the raising of the creative force field on the Earth so that the balance of feminine and masculine can be reached yet again.

"It is my responsibility to bring the creative forces of the universe, which happen to be feminine forces, back to the universe, instill them in their neutral point, imbue them with the light of God and remind all souls, male and female, about our need to return to the creative forces. Until and unless we learn to support, respect and revere the feminine forces, we cannot make headway.

"I have been called in the literature the 'virgin' goddess, but this is not exactly accurate because I have taken human form on Earth. In these human forms over the centuries, I have born children, many children. Indeed, some of you readers have been my children in past lifetimes. "

Quan Yin was the Chohan of the Seventh Ray. In the decade of the 1950s when Earth and humanity were going through great post-war physical and spiritual changes, she passed on the directorship of this violet ray to Saint Germain to prepare for the coming of the next golden age and the souls of the Seventh Ray who hold the light and the wisdom necessary for the dawning of this golden age.

She is devoted to helping the souls whose lineage of light is of the Seventh Ray; these souls are perhaps more familiarly known as Indigo Children. The name arises from the predominant indigo color in the energy field or aura of these highly evolved souls who have been coming to Earth in large numbers since the early 1970s. There have been Indigos here before this, however. Mahatma Gandhi was an Indigo. So was the renowned healer Edgar Cayce.

The mission of the souls of the Seventh Ray is to spread their light on Earth to raise the vibration of the collective consciousness of humanity and to assist Mother Earth to raise her own vibration as a planet. Theirs is a rescue mission to assist all souls to remember that we are united in God and that we are all children of God. For this change to happen, Quan Yin says, we must be shaken up; we must enter into the unknown, into new paradigms and mindsets to allow a new golden age to dawn.

Quan Yin was the first ascended being I ever channeled, and that was in 1989. But I was introduced to her before this when someone else channeled Quan Yin and this gentle ascended master told me then to clear my life of everything that was in the way of my spiritual growth because we had work to do together.

She told me that I had walked with her on Earth in different lifetimes. Perhaps this is why I find her energy so familiar and easy to channel.

Let Go and Let God

Quan Yin, channeled May 14, 2003

I invite you to open your heart. I invite you to set aside your anger... Let go and let God...

My Children of Light, I am Quan Yin. It is my pleasure to be asked to offer my prayer of hope and blessing to all the people of the world at this time of great changes.

As the Mother of Compassion, the energies of Quan Yin and Lord Buddha are vastly sent to the Earth and humankind. Beams of light from my heart and from Lord Buddha's heart are bombarding our beloved planet Mother Earth as we speak to bring you back to loving compassion, to assist you in opening your hearts in seeing the love that the masters and the sainted beings of light feel for you and to see our extended auras beckoning you to walk in our direction and in the direction of the light.

As the spokesperson for the energies of mercy and compassion, I invite you to open your heart. I invite you to set aside your anger, your fears, your negativity, your greed, and move away from pain. Enter into the realm of peace and surrender. Let go and let God.

Never before have you had the opportunity to lose the pain this easily. At this point in the evolution of your souls and the soul of Mother Earth, we are guided to come to you, to all the masses of humanity, and to offer you love and compassion, to take your hand and bring you to a place of peace and harmony.

The chaos will continue around you. The more you imbue yourself in our loving compassion, the greater the chance of attaining peace and harmony. In that peace, you can be a beacon of light, a guiding post for others to follow.

As beings of light, I invite you to feel yourself present and accept to be that guiding light for others. Feel the presence of God within your own heart. Call upon the presence of the I Am

That I Am, God in action, and breathe the breath of light from that magical presence into your own lungs and repeat this process every day, every hour, every moment because in the days to come you will need to be anchored in the power, the wisdom and the love of the I Am That I Am.

For yourself and for all those that you shall guide into the light, the light is awaiting you. You are the beacons of that light. You are the sparks of that light. Become empty vessels and let the light shine through you and reach out to the multitudes.

My children, remember the light.
Remember your own true essence
in the presence of the I Am That I Am.

Become the light. Become the I Am. Become the magical presence and the force of the light. Become the power, the wisdom and the love of the I Am That I Am and know that I am with you with my opened arms to receive you.

I am here upon your asking. I can do a great deal more on your behalf upon your asking than you can do on your own. I can assist you and through my assistance, you can help others. Open your hearts and receive me. Call upon me and I shall be with you at all times everywhere. In your love, I am your mother Quan Yin.

Stay Focused on Hope, Choose Mercy Over Justice

Commentary: This was channeled only a few months before the U.S. sent troops to fight a war in Iraq, which was a time when I and others in my spiritual community were comparing notes about our aches and pains. Some of us were also inexplicably irritable; some of us couldn't sleep at night. We did not realize that we were feeling energetically out of sorts because we were feeling what was about to come about from warfare halfway around the world. We were inadvertently picking up the coming negativity of the war and absorbing it to ourselves.

Quan Yin appeared at this time to explain this phenomenon and instruct us on how to remove ourselves from the conflictive energies that had us in such turmoil. Her guidance is still instructive today. Use it when you feel out of sorts— physically, mentally, and emotionally— and you can't explain why you are feeling this way. Use it in times of turmoil that you have no control over, such as natural disasters (volcanic eruptions, floods, earthquakes and the like) and human-made disasters like war or any other kinds of abuse or violence.

Indigo children are especially sensitive to these kinds of energies, even though the negativity may be physically far distant and they may be consciously unaware of the source of the energies. Please be gentle with your children at such times, and don't blame them or yourself for their difficult conduct.

Quan Yin, channeled July 28, 2002

My dear children, I am Quan Yin. I would like to spend a few minutes giving you some tools.

The world is in a state of upheaval. It is important that you **stay grounded**. There are times when you will feel as though things are getting worse rather than better. Those are the times when you have to be focused on hope. There will be times when you find people around you in a frenzy. Those are the times that you need to be focused in will power.

Have light colored flowers around you— very light pinks, whites. Roses will serve you. Gardenias, if you could keep them in your climate, would hold a very high intensity of truth and purity.

Wear white around your heart as much as possible.

If you need protection from the environment, wear black but wash it as soon as the occasion has come and gone because it does absorb to itself a lot of dross. So, if you wear a black outfit once, don't think it is still clean. Wash it so that the dross can be released. [Quan Yin is saying that black clothing protects but it takes on negative energy and therefore must be cleaned. You can clean the material by washing it or saging it.]

Wear pearls whenever you can. Pearls will bring you purity. Even if you keep a strand of pearls under your pillow at night, it will help purify your system. [That is, your physical body and your energy field].

Have the energies of amethyst close to you. If you can, **collect some amethyst and some rose quartz** crystals and place them under your beds. In this way, you are focusing your energies on love and on higher vibrations. Amethyst will reconnect you to the higher realms. Rose quartz will keep your heart open and transmute the energies of dross around you.

You have heard enough times that you are what you eat. **Avoid fiery foods** and if you are mixing fiery foods, those with deep colors, then dilute them so they turn into a much lighter color.

Foods with tomato sauce will not be agreeable to your digestive system; it will have a lot of fire. A little bit of it is fine. Too much of it will give you trouble.

Avoid spices. **Avoid garlic**. Although it is a good purifying essence, it holds a very high concentration of transmutational energies and this is why in many diets, they offer you garlic. But to eat great quantities of garlic is as though you are asking the universe to bring you transmutation, to bring you fire, fire that burns. [At other times, however, when you need to detoxify and purify your body, it is good to add a lot of garlic to your diet.]

Eat grounding foods. **Eat root vegetables**. Eat potatoes if you need grounding. Incorporate green vegetables, **a lot of green vegetables.** They will protect you against the energies of violence, the energies of fear. Broccoli, lemons, limes.

You may find a new craving for salt. Salt is grounding.

You may feel a lack of desire for certain foods. Heed your body. **Do as your body tells you**.

Try and **drink the juice of root vegetables**. Carrot juice will be very good for you. Beet juice — you only need half a cup and you can mix it, and although it is red and it is a warm food, it is a root vegetable and it holds the energy of the heart.

If you take half a cup of beet juice and mix it in a glass of water, you will have a very light colored pink potion. It will attract to you the energies of love. In the same way that colors vibrate those energies, those colors in the foods vibrate those energies inside of you.

If you can use [make] juices, add celery juice and cucumber juice to carrot and to beet. One stalk of celery [and a] quarter of a cucumber is sufficient for one juice drink. Two carrots— that will make one drink.

One small beet, one stalk of celery, a quarter of a cucumber will give you a half cup of juice. You dilute that with water and drink it immediately. Even if you do that twice a week, it will help you.

It doesn't serve you to make a great quantity of juice and place it in a cool place. It is the freshness that is important. It is not necessary for you to take large quantities in dense form. Diluting what I have discussed in water will help its absorption through your body. It will create a shield around your body that will protect you.

The Earth is in need of burning its dross. The human consciousness has chosen to do this, in spite of all efforts, through harm, damage and violence. It's a choice that has been made by the free will of humankind. There will be bloodshed. There will be a loss of souls.

As much as you can, gather with others whenever you hear of another disaster. **Create vortices of energies for the lost souls that leave the energy field of Earth**. All you need to do is to sit together in prayer and invoke the ascended masters and ask for a vortex of energy to be created whereby the disembodied souls who have lost their way can then enter the vortex and be taken to light. Call upon Archangel Michael and his legions to assist in the process of taking the lost souls on their journey home to light.

Protect yourselves from those who will move to the energies of frenzy. Protect yourselves from those who are giving in to hopelessness. Protect yourself from those whose energies are vibrating lower frequencies.

Stay in the energies of truth.

Call upon the three masters who have offered themselves in assistance to the consciousness of humanity— Hilarion, El Morya, and St. Germain. Call upon them with every breath. Call upon the Brotherhoods of Light and ask that the impact of the inflictions be reduced as much as possible so that in your own reality, you would only have to go through a lower vibration of damage and destruction rather than a higher intensity of damage and destruction.

Understand that there is only so much that the masters can do; but even then, what they can do, even if it is small, will be of great help. From your own point of view, **constantly call upon assistance from the higher realms**. Call upon Michael and his legions for the energies of mercy.

As much as possible, **ask for mercy rather than justice**. If justice were to be served, many heads would have to roll. Many untruths would have to come to the surface. Great destruction will result.

It is best to be focused on the energies of mercy. It is best to be focused on the energies of compassion. Focus your intention on compassion and mercy, and purity and love. **Focus your will to remain hopeful. Focus your will to remain truthful.**

Keep pearls close to you. Wear white around your heart. Eat foods that are simple and grounding. Avoid hot spices. Avoid fiery foods. Avoid giving in to the thoughts of violence. Avoid giving in to the thoughts of justice. Focus on mercy. Focus on love. Focus on compassion. Call upon Michael and his legions. Call upon the Buddhas and bodhisattvas of compassion. Light candles and imbue them with the energies of compassion, love, truth, hopefulness and will-fullness.

[To imbue a candle, take it in your hands and pray over it, calling on the angels and other beings of light, and ask them to assist you to will these energies of compassion and so forth into the candle.]

My children, I am an aspect of the Divine Mother. I have given my life in Heaven in order to serve you on Earth. I gave up the life in Heaven so that I can lead you and hold your hands on the way on this journey to find God within.

My eyes are focused on everyone's heaven here on Earth. My heart is set on showing everyone heaven here on Earth. It can be attained. It will be done. It has already taken position. That alternate reality is a truth you will walk upon. It's a path that will unfold before you. It will be rocky at first. Things will unfold very differently from what humanity can imagine.

But if you throw thoughts of justice, if you throw thoughts of 'an eye for an eye,' if you throw thoughts of serving the self, centering one's focus on the self, accumulating a better life for the self at the cost of others, this is what will happen:

The energies that are sent to Earth at this time are of the kind whereby, what you are will be magnified. What you think will be magnified. What you do will be magnified.

Think goodness and hope. Do what is in your truth. Bring to yourself compassion and love. Think of serving in compassion and love. Put service before all else. Let service be your mantra.

Let purity be your path. Let your focus be upon hopefulness and willfullness. Let the future be filled with love, peace and hope. Call upon the Buddhas and bodhisattvas of compassion.

This is the time we bring our energies as close to you as you will desire it. Desire that closeness.

My children, in your love, I am your Mother Quan Yin.

Entering Into Oneness

Quan Yin, channeled October 29, 1997

God has now given you a dispensation to clear all karma and to begin the return journey home.

My children of light, I am Quan Yin. I wish to explain to you the essence of the universal law of cause and effect and to compare it with the law of divine love.

The separation between God and humankind began out of the free will of God and humankind. When God decided to separate itself from the totality of its being, it became fragmented; therefore, it separated from its original essence.

At that point, God commanded: "Let there be light."

From God's own self, light was sent to the four corners of the universe, reaching to the fragments that God had given free will. As each fragment used its free will and made universe decisions, karma was created.

Karma means action. A set of rules to measure these actions was given. Through this, the law of cause and effect or karma came to exist.

Before then, we lived in God unity. In that state, all actions and decisions come from the same source, from the heart of God. And all is based on love. This constitutes the universal law of divine love.

As the universal law of divine love gave way to divine karma, each action became separate from its source, causing a specific effect. This created the wheel of birth and death, and because the effect of some actions spread over longer than one lifetime, reincarnation came about.

Sometimes a human being spends many lifetimes reaping the effect of actions caused in a previous lifetime. The return journey home was therefore delayed until humanity had completed the course of one's created karma.

God has now given you a dispensation to clear all karma and to begin the return journey home. According to this dispensation, we will return to the universal law of divine love. Our actions and the cause and effect of these actions will only be measured according to divine love.

The compassionate heart of the one God who is tired of waiting, separate from its children, has brought this dispensation. Help and assistance is brought to humanity through divine love. The slate is cleaned of karma.

Under this law, the mercy and compassion of God is given to humanity through the masters and holy beings, as well as the angels and archangels.

Now you can offer your karma back to God through the intercession of these beings. You can remove yourself from the wheel of rebirth and death and enter into oneness.

Linear time and space no longer need to affect you. The ascended masters, the legions of angels and archangels, guides and guardians are constantly present to assist you. They are ready to cut the cords of karma, relieve you of pain and assist you to return to oneness in the heart of God.

You can only achieve oneness when you are healthy and whole again, when you completely remember that you are one with God, when you release the fragments and return into union.

***I urge you, my children, to heal yourself.
I give you tools to commence the healing process.
I give you mantras to clear your energy bodies.
I offer you the clearing of your body, mind and emotions through instant healing.***

Now is the time to let the mind release old thought forms, beliefs and behaviors.

The mind needs to be reminded of the new dispensation and to release the old ways.

Instantaneous healing can come if only the mind would believe it. The physical body is the vehicle. By mere intention, you can bring healing and wholeness to body, mind and spirit.

The only reason that you may not feel instantaneous healing is because the mind gets in the way and diverts back to the old habits.

God in its divinity has forgiven all. Now it is time for you to forgive yourself. God has let go and you are still holding on. This is no longer necessary. God is offering you mercy. Mercy means that assistance is given to humanity out of love, not out of the merits that you earn.

You no longer need to concern yourself with whether you deserve it or not. God has given it to you. Take it and be grateful for the gifts of mercy.

There is a great world of joy waiting for you. You are still holding on to the pain and sorrow of the past. Past is history. The history is changing.

You made an intention to be relieved of suffering and God heard your plea and gave you this new dispensation with great mercy. You don't believe that you have received this great gift. You are still living the past and therefore are missing not just the present but even what the future holds for you.

Make an intention to let go of the past right here, right now.

Together we can work to begin on the new path, the path of light. In the company of all guides and angels, make this intention and ask that karma be removed and pain and suffering be left behind.

Repeat this with me:

I remove all karma, all pain, all misery from my entire being.

I forgive myself and all others for everything that deserves forgiveness.

I remove all the cords and residue of negative energies and I offer them to God for transmutation.

I remove all lack from my being.

I stand before God in total health and wholeness, desiring and demanding union.

I command all my guides, my guardians, my angels and archangels, the masters, my higher self, and my God-self to bring me God unity.

I demand God unity and ask for assistance in obtaining it.

I receive God unity in this now.

And so it is.

It is done. Amen.

My children, believe that it is this simple. When you achieve focus and you believe in the truth of this discourse, all will return to union.

If you believe one repetition of this prayer is sufficient, then say it once. If you do not believe this, then repeat the prayer as many times as necessary until you can believe it fully and completely. This is my promise to you.

Prayer to Return to Light and Release Fear

Quan Yin, channeled January 9, 2001

Commentary: Use this invocation at all times. Clear your minds of all fear. Bring your body to a state of groundedness. Still your emotions. Speak these words with full love, authority and power. Fill your heart with love. Move yourself to a place of centered focus and conscious awareness that you are light and begin. Take a deep breath, sit or stand comfortably and say the mantra out loud or say it silently but with full intent.

I AM That I AM.

Pure light I AM.

Point of light I AM.

White light I AM.

From the point of light where God and I are one, I call upon my guides, my guardian angels, the masters and mistresses of light, the high beings of light to release me from all fear.

From the point of light where God and I are one, I call forth the assistance of all my guides, my guardian angels, the masters and mistresses of light and I ask for the release of all pain and suffering.

From the point of light where God and I are one, I ask for the release of all fear.

From the point of light where God and I are one, I ask for the release of all lack.

From the point of light where God and I are one, I call forth the energies of pure white light.

I Am the embodiment of compassion and love.

I Am the embodiment of joy and light.

I Am the embodiment of peace and harmony.

Pure light I AM.

Point of light I AM.

White light I AM.

I AM That I AM.

Understanding God Unity

The Little Girl Who Forgot

Quan Yin, channeled October 28, 1997

I can no longer take the pain away for you and tell you to forget, for the time has come for you to remember that there is no need for duality. The time for God unity has come.

My children of light, I am Quan Yin. It is my desire at this point to deliver to you a sweet story. Let me take you back to 600 years. The land is China. The child is a four-year-old girl wearing Chinese robes, her feet tightly bound in wooden clogs.

She is sitting in front of a landscape of beautiful jasmines and gardenias in a small garden with a water fountain and a pond. She holds a thought. The thought in her mind is a question, and the question is: *How did I get here?*

The child has no recollection of separation; the child only remembers union. The child also is capable of great clairvoyance. When people talk to her or to one another, and are not sincere in their words, she can see that. She not only reads their minds, she hears their words, and she wonders why there is a separation between what their heart feels and what their mouths speak.

She enjoys spending time on her own by the lily pond and also with her great grandmother, a wise women of many years. The little girl loves holding the wrinkled face of the grandmother in her hands and kissing her.

The grandmother smells like jasmines and gardenias, and she has a golden-pink halo around her body that shines when she speaks, and she only speaks the truth. She doesn't speak often, for there are so many words of truth to be spoken, and on a daily basis the nature of truth does not change; the truth is always the truth. It remains that way over eons of time.

In her childlike knowing, the little girl understands that she can ask the great grandmother about the nature of duality and how she ended up in this place of separation. And she can also ask about how it is that everyone around her does not speak the truth that the great grandmother speaks, and why they hold one feeling in their hearts, why they speak of a different feeling with their mouths.

When she puts this question to her great grandmother, the old woman smiles her knowing smile and embraces the child. She places her index finger on the child's third eye and speaks these words: "For the sake of love, forget, my child, the truth that you know, for this land and the people are not ready to hear the truth."

At once, the clairvoyance and the ability to read minds and words leave the girl. She becomes a happy joyful child, who is only concerned with little childlike pleasures. No longer is she concerned with worldly matters; no longer does she carry the burden of spiritual wisdom upon her shoulders.

So, my children of light, I ask you this question, after having told the story: What would you do in the place of the great grandmother? What would you have done had you been given the choice of answering the question and leaving the burden of such great wisdom upon a four year old?

Would you have allowed her to become a child of that time or would you have allowed her to maintain her gifts and to continue the way she was until such time that she became an adult and was able to understand and realize the nature of things through hardship, through pain, through trial and error?

I leave the question to you, but I will tell you why I have brought this subject before you. Envision yourself as a child of four, and imagine me as your great grandmother 600 years ago when you asked me: Why the duality? Why the separation?

Imagine I told you that now it is no longer the time for you to forgive and forget, my child.

The time is now for you to know, my children of light. I can no longer take the pain away for you and tell you to forget, for the time has come for you to remember that there is no need for duality. The time for God unity has come.

In understanding the nature of God unity, you have to thoroughly experience the nature of duality. You have to experience the pain of knowing that duality no longer serves you. You have to be given just a taste of union— union of the one with the One, as One. And now is the time.

The time has come for duality to end. It is no longer possible for the great grandmother to hold and embrace you and take your pain away by making you forget. It is time for remembrance. It is time for recording, recapturing, realizing, realigning, recreating, and rebirthing.

There are pains to go through as the process of rebirthing takes place. In the process of rebirthing, realize that your physical body is changing. Realize that what served you during duality in your physical body and mind shall no longer serve you during unity.

Therefore, you will experience many pains and discomforts in your physical body, even as you exercise various healing modalities. Even as you get together in groups and raise the energies, you will experience extremes of backache, extremes of headache.

You experience that your eyes are losing their focus, that your vision is blurred, especially after you have done a great deal of energy work. You notice that your calves are aching, your knees, your ankles. You notice sharp pains going up and down your body. Women will feel this most specifically on their left side, men most specifically on their right side. All of this is very common to the process of rebirthing.

The physical body that you have used for the last hundreds of years during the time of duality and forgetfulness no longer serves you. This physical body is changing, it is mutating, it is being reborn, it is recreating itself.

You are the prototypes, the role models; you are the experimental samples. Therefore, when the pain comes to you, accept it. Do not fear it.

And as you accept it, call your guides and your angels. Call upon Michael and myself Quan Yin, or our beloved Melchizedek or any other guide or guardian you choose to call upon. Call upon the Prime Creator. Call upon any being of the angelic or archangelic realm or call the masters.

Tell them that the pain is unbearable. Describe the pain. Explain what you need in order to make the pain easier, and then say to them, "If it is my highest wisdom that you take this pain away or at least reduce it to a bearable minimum, please do so. It is in this area and it feels this way, and I wish it to be removed from this area or to be reduced."

Although this may help you, know still that you will certainly feel the pain. It is not because I am the prophet of doom that I tell you this. You will realize that it is an integral part of your process of rebirthing, of your process of growing to adulthood. Right now you are a child of two years old. In a matter of minutes, in a matter of hours, you will grow from a child of two to a full-grown adult being. How can your bones, your cells, your tissue bear such growth in such a period?

This growth was meant to take place over 35 or 40 years of your time and now it is taking place in minutes.

This is only an analogy I am giving to you. When you make your ascension and your Earth completes the process of becoming a star, when you rend the veil and appear on the other side in the new octave of existence, in the new realm and dimension of reality, even then you are only a child of two. You will be trying to grow and absorb the things going on around you, and even then, you need to learn to crawl before you can walk.

In any event, it will help you to know that you are not alone, that your body is not giving you problems; you do not need to rush to your doctor. Should you desire to go and see a doctor, let your mind be peaceful. See the physician, but do not be disappointed when they find nothing wrong with you; be glad that nothing was found and remind yourself that these are the mutational changes, these are the mutational pains that your body is going through, and everything is exactly as it should be.

If I had a way to take away this pain for you, believe me, I would have done so. If there was a way to make this change easier for you, I would be the first to make that possible. We are already in this present moment trying very hard to make things easier for you.

Still, it might help to think of yourselves as if you were part of an experiment being conducted for the first time. As each one of you experiences the effects of this experiment, your reactions and responses are noted and taken into consideration for those who will follow. The experiment will then be adjusted to become more and more comfortable for each group that goes after you.

Those of you who are experiencing these pains at the present moment are not only doing this for yourselves, but you are having this experience so that the entire planet can achieve critical mass and complete the process of becoming a star being. You are doing this so that everyone can be reborn as star children.

As you work toward tearing the veil, you are building inside every cell of your being the 12 strands of DNA. The [Indigo] children that have been born in the last three years have been born with 12 strands of DNA intact. You, on the other hand, are rebuilding and reconstructing these strands of DNA inside your body as you go along. As you continue the process of mutation, you rebuild this body; you change, mutate and elevate your body in order to integrate it with the light body.

As you simultaneously elevate your physical body to meet with the light body and lower the light body to fit into the dense physical body, this process of integration will cause you to experience some growing pains. It is with great pleasure that I suggest to you to go through these pains knowing that you are the first ones to have this experience. It is always a great honor and a great pleasure to be the first ones to have a brand new experience, is it not?

With that, I remind you that at any point if you feel the pain is becoming unbearable, at any point you feel the discomfort is more than you deserve, call upon the masters, call upon the guides, call upon all the beings of light. Call upon your guides and tell them the nature of the pain, and tell them how you wish it to be reduced. Ask, "If it is my highest wisdom, please reduce the pain. If it is my highest wisdom, please release the pain completely so that I can have this wonderful experience joyfully."

Even when you have to have the pain, add joy to the pain. Enjoy the pain. Understand that it is part and parcel of the process that you are going through.

And so it is.

Mantra and Dance of Peace

Quan Yin, channeled May 24, 2002

My children of light, I am Quan Yin. I would like to offer you a lovely dance. I would very much appreciate it if you would light a candle in the name of peace in the world. This dance is given for peace on Earth. This is a peace dance and a peace mantra.

Before starting to sing the mantra, let everyone go around the circle and say out loud that your intention is for peace on Earth. And then go within and say your personal prayer for this ceremony. Then begin the mantra.

Understand that before you say the mantra, you are coming from the world of duality and you find yourself in separation from God. It is important therefore that sound be vibrated by everyone who is present in this ceremony to clear the energy field of your body, your intentions and the energy grid of the Earth where you are standing.

Once you begin the mantra, you are the elements of God. When each person says the mantra, you are speaking from that space where you and God are one. You are ultimately one with God and you perform this ceremony or dance from that space.

Mantra

From the point of light where the Undifferentiated Source and I are one, I command peace on Earth.

From the point of light where the Undifferentiated Source and I are one, I imbue the Earth with peace.

From the point of light where the Undifferentiated Source and I are one, I fill the hearts of all souls with peace.

From the point of light where the Undifferentiated Source and I are one, I fill the life force of this planet, Mother Earth, with peace.

From the point of light where the Undifferentiated Source and I are one, I fill the collective consciousness of this planet, Mother Earth, with peace.

I command all bodies, all minds, and all souls to rest in peace.

In the Light of the Source I AM.

As the Light of the Source I AM.

From the Light of the Source I AM.

Light I AM. Love I AM. Bliss I AM. Peace I AM.

I AM. I AM. I AM.

So it is. It is done. Amen.

Dance

Imagine two triangles of light merged together to make a six-pointed star. Ideally there are 14 persons in attendance, two people at each point representing the angels and two in the center representing the Heavenly Father/Earthly Mother. If you do not have 14 people, you may use crystals to anchor the points.

Imagine the star in your mind's eye, or map it out on the floor and move around the grid on your own.

Read aloud the entire mantra once in the first position. Repeat line by line moving from point to point, and finally back to the original point, you say the entire mantra one more time.

The mantra in and of itself is a powerful tool of transformation.

Point 1 North Angels of Sun and Power
Point 2 Northeast Angels of Water and Love

Point 3 Southeast Angels of Air and Wisdom
Point 4 South Angels of Earth and Eternal Life
Point 5 Southwest Angels of Life and Work
Point 6 Northwest Angels of Joy and Peace
Point 7 Center Heavenly Father & Earthly Mother

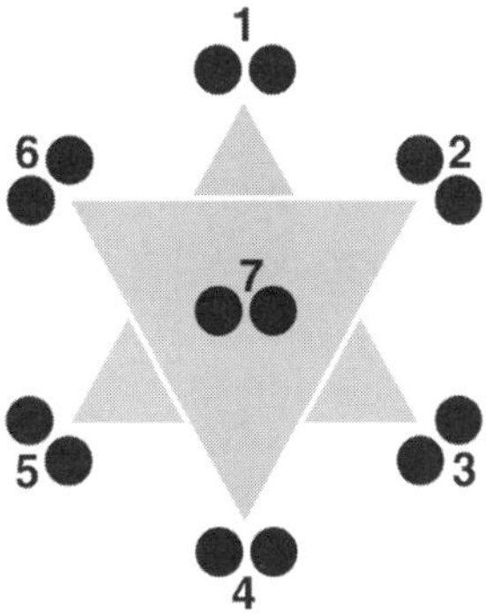

To Begin...

- Take your positions— two people and/or a person and a crystal at each of the six points and in the center [which makes seven].

- Take a moment to call in the 14 angels and all beings you wish to be present. Take a moment to go inside and offer your personal intention on the inner into the grid.

- Then each person says aloud an intention for peace on Earth.

- Together, chant OM once or as many times as you feel necessary.

- Then everyone repeats the entire mantra together at the starting points.

- Proceed clockwise to the next point, at which time you stop and repeat only the first line of the mantra.

- Continue on to the next point, repeating only the second line of the mantra.

- Continue around the circle until you have said the entire mantra completely. (Twelve stanzas will bring you back to your starting point).

- At your end point, everyone say the complete mantra together to complete the ceremony.

If you are in the center of the grid, your movements coincide with the four directions. Begin facing North, then turn East, South, West, and so on for each line of the mantra. You should make a total of 3 rotations (12 stanzas).

Throughout the entire repetition of the mantra, imagine the entire grid spinning like a hologram. The intention of this dance is to bring prosperity and peace, for our individual prosperity will make us peaceful and world peace will make us prosperous.

Good luck! And remember that you are doing this ceremony as part of a prosperity exercise. Remember that there is peace that comes with prosperity and prosperity that comes with peace. When you have peace of mind, you can focus. You put your energies into something constructive. And when you have prosperity, you can put that peace into service. The two go hand in hand.

With great love, with great joy for being here with you, and with the hope that I will be with each of you in your own homes, your own circles, your own groups.

By helping others to do this ceremony, you will heal the Earth and you will bring peace on Earth. May this peace be upon you and your hearts. With great love in the company of all masters and all angels, I am your mother Quan Yin.

So it is.

Saint Germain

Saint Germain is an ascended master who came to be known by his present name because of his incarnation as the eighteenth century French count Comte de Saint Germain. No one seemed to know his origin or his parents. Some accounts claim that he appeared and reappeared for more than 300 years in the same body as Comte de Saint Germain.

Saint Germain is the Chohan of the Seventh Ray, the violet ray. He has had many prominent lifetimes in service to the light, among them as Saint Francis of Assisi, Francis Bacon and Saint Joseph, father of the ascended master Jesus and the husband of Mary.

Saint Germain has been deeply involved with both the protection of America and the creation of the United States as a truly free country. He played a major role in drafting the U.S. Constitution. He has said that a new age will dawn in the land of the free, and this will be the seventh golden age.

Saint Germain has brought forth a large body of material known as the Saint Germain Series, channeled through two highly evolved souls, Guy W. Ballard (1878-1939) and his wife Edna (1886-1971). Saint Germain gave them the spiritual names of Godfré Ray King and Lotus Ray King. When the Ballards made their ascension, they left behind 18 volumes, some published only recently. (www.saintgermain foundation. org and www.saintgermainpress.com).

My first encounter with Saint Germain was in the early years when I first started channeling. One day in a vision I received while meditating, I saw a very regal man who was bedecked in ceremonial robes of mostly purple and gold. He also wore jewelry around his neck and fingers.

Never having even heard of him before, I did not know who he was. He introduced himself to me as Count Saint Germain, and then he began a discourse on the ways of the universe and the evolution of the soul.

Once I became acquainted with his energy, I began to channel him in the presence of small groups. After several years of working intensely with him, I began to see him less. He came occasionally, and when he came, it was to speak to only specific people present during the channeling.

When a studen— or as Saint Germain says, a *chela*, which is student in Sanskrit— is ready, the master will come and imbue his energies. When Saint Germain feels that he has brought a student to a certain level, he steps back for other masters to step in. As the student evolves, Saint Germain reappears.

Over the years I've learned that Saint Germain is extremely precise and very focused. He does not use extra words to explain himself.

The Consuming Violet Flame

Saint Germain, channeled May 14, 2003

Give us a chance to help you and together we shall fill the Earth and the consciousness of all souls with pure bright white light...

My dear hearts, I am Saint Germain. For hundreds of years I have worked on behalf of humanity and Mother Earth to bring the peace and the light of the I Am That I Am to Earth and to open the hearts of all souls to their own true essence in the presence of the I Am That I Am.

I have made great efforts to leave large bodies of literature, devotional prayers, decrees, invocations, dispensations, to bring you to light, to assist you, to anchor the three-fold flame of power, wisdom and love in your hearts and in the heart of your Mother Earth.

The energies of your sister planet Venus are open for humanity to receive and benefit from. Venus is much like your older sister. If you could only dream of setting foot where Venus has left off, you will be in good hands.

For this reason, all the ascended masters who have been involved in the construction and the spiritual evolution of Venus are now present in the atmosphere of Earth and willing to give assistance to all those who ask for it.

Simply call upon the ascended masters from Venus and upon Saint Germain, the patron, the Chohan of the Seventh Ray, and ask for the transmutation of all negativity through the violet consuming flame of love that burns in Venus and burns in the heart core of all the enlightened star systems of this entire universe.

By asking the Consuming Violet Flame to release all negativity from all your lifetimes, you will lighten your load and you will reach to the light faster and your journey will be an easier one.

Now is the time to constantly call upon the presence of the I Am That I Am and the transmutational vibrations of the Violet Consuming Flame from the heart of divine love, from the sacred core of the central Sun of this entire universe.

The central Sun of this universe is opening its gateways to you. This has been given to you through the intercession of the planet Venus and the ascended masters who work with your planet and Venus. Envision Venus providing a filter that will prevent you from being exposed to the extremes of light.

This filter is mainly constructed on ultra-violet energies that are brought forth through the Violet Consuming Flame.

These ultra-violet energies reflecting the light from the central Sun will clear and cleanse your planet Earth and the karma of every individual soul, from incarnation to incarnation, until such point that karma is no more and the universal law of karma or cause and effect is no longer necessary or applicable for Earth or humankind.

This is then replaced with the universal law of divine love which is the order in higher evolved planets and star systems which have become enlightened— such as Venus, your older sister, or Jupiter, a much older brother or perhaps a great uncle, and obviously the Sun of your own solar system, which is the greatest and the most highly evolved star of this entire system.

Call upon the masters and beings of light from these planets and star systems to come to your assistance in the name and in the presence of the I Am That I Am.

Call upon the presence of the Violet Consuming Flame to release your load of many incarnations worth of karma and cause and effect and clean your slate from all debts, karmic or chosen by your soul on its journey from the heart of God to the depth of darkness at this point where you are about to make the turn in the direction of the return journey home.

At this point, you do not need to take back with you all the burdens that you have carried from the beginning of time through the depth of darkness.

As you turn around and face the light, know that to return to the light, you only need your heart, your emotions, your joy, your happiness and your wholeness in body, mind and spirit.

We can help you find your happiness, your joy and your wholeness. At this point, we can assist you in pointing you to the direction of light and showing you your journey homebound. We can do this only if you choose to ask for it. We cannot give you assistance unless you ask for assistance.

The law of your planet requires that assistance be given when it is asked for because the law of your planet requires that it be a free-will soul. That means your own free will supercedes any will that may be externally imposed upon it, good, bad or indifferent. There are exceptions to these rules, but for the most part, your free-will planet requires us to wait until you ask for assistance and to only give you assistance when we have been asked for it.

I, as your older brother, ask you to remember to request our assistance.

Remember to call upon us to bring you help and guidance. Remember to call upon us even in moments where you believe what you wish for is unworthy of asking. Ask and call upon us even over matters that seem trivial to you. It is in the details that sometimes you spend the most amount of time finding yourself lost and confused.

In general principles, most of you are aware that we are on our journey homebound. The question is: Which fork on the road will you choose to take? And which of these paths that are offered to you will be of greatest benefit and of the highest interest of your soul's evolution?

So, you see, it is in details that you need our guidance, and we can bring you the greatest guidance merely by the fact that you have asked for it.

We have your point of view because we know your heart. We have God's point of view because we are connected to God's heart. We can relate these two points of view to one another, not because God needs a translator but because you need a translator.

And we can play this role as an older sibling would for, after all, this is what we are. We have followed the same path, only we have done it a few eons before you did and we have learned from taking the same steps in the same direction, seeing the results for ourselves.

This is an open-ended story for you from where your standpoint is. This is a story we have written and concluded from where our standpoint is. So, if you want to know the last chapters of this book, all you need to do is to ask us. We would be happy to guide you to the final conclusion that will serve you, humanity, the Earth and this entire universe with greatest light.

There are many ways that you can write these ending chapters of your book of life. The choice is yours, whether you would write it in 144 chapters or you would write it in 12.

If you so choose to call upon us to assist you in finding the path, the path of straight and narrow, the path with greatest light, the most victorious and glorious path of light, we are here at your service.

Give us a chance to help you and together we shall fill the Earth and the consciousness of all souls with pure bright white light.

In your love, I am Saint Germain.

Invocation for Protection of Self and Property

Commentary: Stand in the center of the room or yard or whatever physical property you wish to protect. Extend your arms out in front of you.

Saint Germain, channeled September 28, 2002

Take a deep breath. Focus your energies in your solar plexus. Envision in the center of your solar plexus a disc, a disc of gold and white. The disc is becoming larger, extending out to the point where it is about a foot outside of your body, spinning counter-clockwise, beaming golden light.

Repeat after me:

I am the perfection of pure white light.

I am the perfected vibration of pure white light.

I am the illumination of pure white light.

I invoke a bubble of light over this entire house and property.

I am the illumination of light over this entire house and property.

I am the illumination of light over this entire house and property.

I am the illumination of light over this entire house and property.

I am the mighty presence of God ever present in the center of this property.

I am the mighty presence of God present in the center of this property.

I am the mighty presence of God present in the center of this property.

I am the mighty presence of God present in the center of this property.

I am the mighty presence of God ever present in the center of this property.

I am the perfected mighty presence of God ever present in the center of this property.

I am the perfected mighty presence of God ever present in the center of this property.

I am the perfected mighty presence of God ever present in the center of this property.

I am the perfected mighty presence of God ever present in the center of this property.

Now, say it until you believe it and don't forget the words— *I am the perfected mighty presence of God ever present in the center of this property.*

When you fully embody this invocation, you will see the presence of God in the form of a bubble of light that illuminates the entire property.

But you must say it until you become it— *I am the perfected mighty presence of God ever present in the center of this property. I am the perfected mighty presence of God ever present in the center of this property. I am the perfected mighty presence of God ever present in the center of this property.*

Initiation into the Brotherhoods of the White Lodge

Commentary: The White Lodge is an etheric or energetic retreat of certain ascended masters— those 'who have attained the highest degrees of light,' according to Metatron. This initiation journey brings us into the presence of the illumined beings of this retreat.

The words of this initiation are imbued with the energies of the White Lodge. Simply by reading them, you come into these energies— how much depends on you, how open you are to receiving them.

As you go on this journey, you may or may not see what Saint Germain describes. You may sense the presence of others around you. Even if you do not see or feel, at a subconscious level, you have been touched by the energies imbued in this communion.

Saint Germain, channeled September 25, 2002

My dear hearts, I am Germain. Hold steady. Come with me on a journey.

I offer you the garment of light. Take it, place it over your head, and let your entire body be illuminated with the beams of light that emanate from the essence of the garment of light. The garment of light has its own consciousness.

As you place this garment around your body, you become invisible. Your body becomes lighter and you are magnetized with the higher realms and dimensions of light.

I wish to take you today to the golden city of God. An initiation has been prepared for you. I wish to offer you initiation into the Brotherhoods of the White Lodge. The mastery that comes to you is well earned. You have desired to become pure light. Your desire has been heard. It is well received and now we must act upon the request for your presence.

Within the golden city and inside initiation chambers, become aware of your body. It is vibrating pure white light. I create a tunnel through the time and space continuum. I become the shield to protect you and I lead you to the golden city.

We are now hovering above the atmosphere of the golden city. Take note. Consider the surroundings. A golden gate of light appears before you. I command the golden gate to open. We all enter inside.

You will see many beings of light, fully illuminated. They look like crystal balls emanating light. These are the ascended masters and mistresses of light. Receive your blessing in their presence. Observe the multitudes who have come to receive you.

Let us walk together to the great hall. At the entrance of the great hall, every one of us receives our ceremonial cape, our scepters of power, and our spheres of illumination.

The sphere is a sign of your own lineage. The cape is made of [a luminous gossamer] fabric, seamless and in the color that relates to your specific ray. A ceremony is in progress. We together enter into the great hall. The seating is arranged around an oval centerpiece. This is much like an amphitheater. You are guided to your specific seat.

Breathe deeply and anchor yourself in the light as the ceremony begins.

Twelve beings of light take their positions around the oval centerpiece. Everyone now stands in attention. We are in the presence of the great, wise, cosmic being of light.

At the very center of the oval shaped stage, a pillar of light is illuminated and we all begin to recognize the essence of the great, wise, cosmic being materializing.

You will not hear the words. You will only receive the emanations of this cosmic being's pure light. As you receive the emanations, feel yourself leave your body and merge into the essence of the great, wise, cosmic being of light. Merge and unite in oneness and receive from this light the initiation.

Through this initiation, greater understanding will be attained. This understanding is well deserved and fully earned. Open your minds and your hearts to receive.

[Take a few moments to receive and absorb and become illumined with the greatest and purest white light.]

It is time. Bring your energies back into the etheric body of light that is enrobed in the garment of light sitting in the amphitheater. We will now return.

The transmission of light from the great cosmic being is now removing its essence. The pillar of light is now lifting.

We may now return. Back at the entrance you will give back your cape, your scepter and your sphere. Their imprint will stay with you even after you have returned to your physical bodies. You may use these tools to attain higher understanding and to reunite with your own higher essence, and your I AM presence.

I bring you back to your physical bodies.

I bid you great love. With great joy, I am your brother Saint Germain.

God grant that the light of unity may envelope the whole Earth and that the seal —'The Kingdom Is God's'— may be stamped upon the brow of all its peoples.

- Baha'u'llah, founder of the Bahai faith

Melchizedek

Melchizedek is the Universal Logos. Logos in Greek means word. Thus, Melchizedek is The Word. He is the ultimate guardian and the ultimate architect of our universe. *When all things began, the Word already was. The Word dwelt with God, and what God was, the Word was.* (John 1:1)

The Bible discusses a Melchizedek priesthood and links it to Jesus. The authors of the New Testament book of Hebrews complain that we would not understand or believe what can be said about Melchizedek— *About Melchizedek we have much to say, much that is difficult to explain, now that you have grown so dull of hearing.* (Hebrews 5:11)

Hebrews describes Melchizedek thus: "He has no father, no mother, no lineage; his years have no beginning, his life no end. He is like the Son of God: he remains a priest for all time." (Hebrews 7:3)

Melchizedek was the second high being of light that I began to channel. He spoke of his own human incarnations on Earth. He had fond memories of himself as the native American chief Red Feather who left a great legacy of his teachings.

When I next encountered the Indian Chief Red Feather, it was in a vision during a ceremony in Serpent Mound in Ohio, a site that is sacred to Native Americans from all over North America. Chief Red Feather appeared to me in ceremonial robes wearing a headdress of multicolored feathers that extended to the ground. He emanated extreme strength and power, as well as gentleness and wisdom. He gave me words of encouragement and told me to continue to learn about Native American customs and ceremonies.

I later began to channel Chief Red Feather and learned to revere him, much like a long lost great grandfather.

As my work with Melchizedek progressed, he instructed me and others in activating a new energetic grid for our planet. This grid is essential for the new golden age, the seventh one, that has been forecast.

He made great efforts to take us suspended in space (in guided meditations) so that we could see the illumined geometrical grid of light around Venus because this was the model for the ascended Earth's grid. Venus is our older, more spiritually evolved sister planet, according to Melchizedek.

When I first looked at the grid around the Earth, the lines of energy that should have been illuminated looked like grooves or holes. But when the grid was finally activated, in 1997, it was fully charged and pulsating vivid colors of light energy.

The following year, Melchizedek instructed us to travel around the world to ensure that the energy of Earth's grid was connected to the energy in different parts of the world. We did this for three consecutive years, doing grid work around the globe three times.

Sometimes he would appoint (and continues to do so presently) specific individuals to do specific grid work—- one was Fritz, a cat, and another was a dog named Daisy who live in the New Jersey home of my friend Lucille. She led a weekly meditation session at her home, and I joined this group from time to time on the instructions of Melchizedek and other ascended beings who are my guides. Fritz and Daisy were always present during our meditations and visualizations on the grid work. As soon as we gathered for our session, Fritz and Daisy took their places with the rest of us. None of us would have dreamed of taking Fritz's spot on the couch.

Melchizedek charged Fritz and Daisy with guarding the grid.

The honor and respect Melchizedek showed these animals filled my heart and the heart of everyone in the New Jersey meditation group with joy. In fact, all of the ascended masters I have channeled show the same respect for these beings who are not of the human kingdom. In private channelings when someone asks about family members, the ascended being who comes through with guidance discusses not only the children of the family but also the pets.

Time Is of the Essence to Raise the Vibration of Light

Melchizedek, channeled May 14, 2003

You must clean your planet, your spirit bodies, your physical bodies, your emotional bodies...

How fast can we achieve critical mass in raising the vibration of light through the light workers? We have a short time...

My dear hearts, I am Melchizedek. As your Universal Logos, I speak on behalf of all the systems within your universe when I say to you that this time is of great essence and of great importance in the history of your entire universe.

This is a turning point. This is a point where many star systems, galaxies and systems of universes are moving in a direction of spiritual elevation and evolution.

For this reason, and in order to serve the light, that which is not of light is called to return to light and that which refuses to return to light is moved further and further away from the centers of the light, to the recesses and the corners of the vast conglomerate of star systems and galaxies that make our universe and in the spaces between the universes where there is nothing but space.

As these forces move away from the centers of light, the centers are filled much like a cup of nectar with greater light, and the greater light will assist in the elevation of these centers to the next level of spiritual evolution.

While all of this is in progress, you must understand your own position in terms of direction and placing of your planet, your solar system, your galaxy within our universe and our position as a universe amongst other universal bodies and in relation to the cosmos and the central Sun for our cosmos.

If you were to think of all these various systems, spirals of light that sit one next to another around a central force-field, a sphere of light which we call the great central Sun of our cosmos, that would be the core of light and the highest illumination of light that any soul could ever imagine.

Around that central sphere of light, which is the cosmic central Sun, are systems of the cosmos. Around the cosmic systems are systems of omniverses.

Around the multitudes of omniverses are systems of universes. Around the systems of universes are systems of galaxies. Around the systems of galaxies are solar systems.

Within each of those solar systems are planetary systems.

Your planet within its own solar system is a very small system within a very small galaxy within a very small system of galaxies that make our universe, and we are at the edge, one of the edges of this cosmic multitude of light.

This complex picture that I have presented to you is evolving in the direction of greater light, and as the core of this light in the central Sun of the cosmos beams out greater beacons of light, that which is of lower light ripples away from the center and in the direction of the periphery.

As the beams of light from the central core reach out to the peripheries, that which is of lower light goes further and further into the recesses of the spaces between galaxies, solar systems and planets.

Right now lower light and lack of light is being chased fully and completely out of these universal cosmic galactic and planetary systems. What is no longer serving the light has to come to the surface and either merge and join the light or be destroyed by light. Even in its destruction through the light, it returns to the light.

Even on the odd occasion where forces have become so dim that hardly any light can be reached to them, they have an opportunity to return to the light. Even in their annihilation, they return to the light.

Nothing ever is destroyed to nothingness. Everything returns to the light. Even in destruction, there is the return journey to the light.

You may not be aware of this fact, but just as matter changes form and becomes energy, moving from form to non-form, darkness can change its dense form as dark matter and become pure light.

What your scientists have termed black holes are vortices of light pulling the dark forces into their core, turning them back into the light and returning them back into the universal systems. On the other side of every black hole there is a light hole.

The unfortunate ironic truth is that your scientists have not yet invented gadgets and technology that can measure matter moving through the dark hole and coming out the other end as light.

Your present telescopes and various mechanical instruments are not capable of measuring the mass of the dark forces that enter into dark holes and turn into the mass of the universal force as light.

Light is always lighter in weight than darkness, just as a body filled with pain feels heavier than a body filled with light and joy.

Your scientists in their measurements have found out that in order for this entire universe to be standing on its own, there has to be greater mass somewhere to hold it all together.

What they do not know how to achieve is to measure the light and to measure mass-less matter. So far, technology can only measure mass, and it is incapable of measuring mass-less matter.

For this reason, in all their equations, there seems to be mass missing. There seems to be inequality between masses and forces of gravity. There is a question of how can it possibly continue in an orderly fashion where there seems to be mass missing. The missing mass is light.

Light does not have mass in its purest form. It doesn't have form either. For those of you who know how to travel the realms of light, you have already noticed that when you are approached by beings of light, they do not have physical bodies. Their entire force field is a mass of light or even a point of light.

But that point of light is so intense in the beings of light that it vibrates throughout your field [and] you feel the vibration as blinding light. And sometimes you have to protect yourself from the blinding force of that light.

This you have learned from your scriptures and the description of the holy sainted beings who have attained so much light that merely looking at them would make your eyes hurt. This you know from looking into the mass of your Sun, the most enlightened and illuminated body of light that is available to you within your own solar system.

You know that it is dangerous for you to look into the center of your Sun with your naked eye. The light can blind you. The light can be intense.

The light sends out such intense beams that it can fry you to a crisp. It can burn your body made of physical matter because the vibration of light is of much higher intensity than the vibration of your bodies made of matter.

The analogy would be that a crystalline structure such as a diamond is a rock but its molecules vibrate so fast that it becomes clear and sends out beams of light that create kaleidoscopic light shows.

Another piece of rock from the similar family of beings [is] your river rock. The river rock is only different from a piece of diamond in that it is vibrating at molecular structure to a much lower vibration of light. Otherwise, they are both pieces of rock.

One of them you have to throw into a glass window to break it. The other one, you merely scratch the glass window and it will make you a clean cut and break the window for you.

One of them has its power focused on merely sending its beam out. The other one has its power in the force of its mass.

Which one is more potent and powerful? Obviously, the piece of diamond— [by] merely scratching the surface of the glass, it can cut the glass to its core.

In the same way, light can penetrate into the depth of darkness and as the dispensation has gone out from the heart core of this central Sun of this cosmos, which is the most intense and pure light essence you can find in this entire cosmic system, the light is beamed out to all the recesses of your entire cosmic system, from omniverses to universes, to galaxies, to solar systems, to planets and to the spaces in between.

All that is of lower light is running away. On its journey outward running away from the Sun, it has already moved into your various systems because location-wise, you are sitting at the edges of all of these systems.

You must shake yourselves off of these energies. You must clean your planet, your spirit bodies, your physical bodies, your emotional bodies, your mental bodies and the mental bodies of all other kingdoms that reside alongside of you from all these dark and negative forces.

Because you are given the guardianship of this planet, all other kingdoms are under your command— the animal kingdom, which consists of all the animals, birds and all those residing in the seas; the plant kingdom which means all the flowers, every blade of grass, all species of trees and everything that grows with roots and trunks and leaves; and the mineral kingdom which goes from the river rock to the diamonds to the precious stones to semi-precious stones, to not-at-all precious stones to the mere sand that you would make glass with or the sand you would mix with mortar and build your houses.

All of these three kingdoms are given under your command and therefore as the forces of darkness move through, it is your job and your responsibility to be the guardian of these kingdoms and to clear and cleanse these kingdoms from all harm, all darkness, all negativity and all pain.

In order to do so, you must vibrate yourselves, your bodies, your consciousness, your beings, your minds and your emotions to a higher vibration of light so that you can then beam out this light to all around you and to clear and cleanse all the kingdoms that are given in your guardianship with your light.

Those of you who call yourselves light workers are such beacons of light. You have accepted a responsibility greater than the masses.

You, as the elite and the chosen ones, who have made an offering and a sacrifice of your time in service, are responsible to assist all others and the three kingdoms to relieve themselves of all dross and negativity and to move in the direction of light.

You are the spearheads. You are the beacons. You are the antenna that transmits the light from the heart of the solar system, the heart, which goes into the solar system from the heart of the cosmic Sun.

The Sun is now sending higher vibrations of light to your planet. The other planets that are more highly evolved in your solar system are now filtering the light from the Sun, ingesting it, changing it, making it absorbable by you on Planet Earth.

Your beloved Mother Earth is now changing her own heartbeat and because of that, the weather patterns are changing. Because of that, the human emotions are changing.

Your moon, which is the feminine energy, also is filtering the vibrations that come from the Sun and the solar system and the planets that are higher evolved than you are, and sending that filtered light to you.

You have had an unprecedented number of solar and lunar eclipses that have left their marks on your bodies and on the bodies of all the kingdoms as well as the body of your Mother Earth, the planet. These marks are signs of change.

After the impact of these solar and lunar eclipses, weather changes come in extreme forces.

The emotional cleansing of Mother Earth is becoming more and more obvious.

These cleansing rituals will continue, becoming more and more forceful, giving you an opportunity to assist the process of cleansing and relieving yourself and your planet and all the three kingdoms of your planet of all darkness and sinister forces.

Instead of going into fear, moving into panic, going into depression, fearing the worst, the time is now to rise above the expectations and surprise the entire universe with your light, with your discipline, with your discipleship of light, with your obedience to light, with your surrender to light, with your willingness to serve the light, with your joy in becoming the light, with your zest for embodying greater light and for your joining in the evolution in light with all your brothers and sisters of planetary and universal and cosmic systems.

As your Universal Logos, as the guardian for this entire universe, I offer you the Brotherhoods and the Sisterhoods of Melchizedek Light in assistance. I offer you the Brotherhoods and the Sisterhoods of the White Lodge, which consists of the ascended masters who have attained the highest degrees of light.

I offer you the greatest and purest elevation of light. I offer you guidance and assistance to move in the direction of vibrating higher light. I offer you an opportunity to raise your own quotient of light.

In order for you to join the rest of the universe in moving to the core, the quotient of light must increase.

The planet and all souls must raise their vibration of light to a higher elevation. Otherwise, the great light that is being beamed out from the central core of the central Sun of this cosmos will be so intense and so great that it will burn you to a crisp.

In your own solar system, your planet is one who is lagging behind. Besides you, there is only one living existing planet that has not made the move to raise its quotient of light to comply with and to pulse in rhythm with the cosmic heartbeat. Other planets in your solar system who have refused in the great history of the eons in the past have become extinct.

There are telltale signs of the existence of those planets in your solar system whereby the scientists have been able to detect the signs and to believe that there must have been other masses and forces creating the energy of a planetary system that must have become extinct over time.

The reason for their extinction is their refusal to accept the light and to begin to raise their vibration of light to bring the rhythm of the pulse and heartbeat equal to the pulse and heartbeat of other solar planetary galactic bodies.

Because of this, a great deal of attention is given to your planet. A great deal of assistance is given to your planet. A great many dispensations have been issued from many levels, directing the pure white light to your planet through the solar system, through the galactic core, through the universal core, through the cosmic core to raise your vibration in the fastest and the most light-effective way.

What stands in the way of your attaining this light is your consciousness. Not the consciousness of the planet, because she has already consented, even requested, even supplicated to receive this light. The only one whose consciousness has not attained the full conformity, has not come to full obedience of light and the universal and cosmic laws is the consciousness of humankind.

We need more of you light workers to open your hearts, to offer your lives in service of awakening other souls to join the light. As with anything that abides the normal laws of your planet and this system of planets, once you achieve critical mass, the rocket boost of the formation of the mass will take the rest of humanity and the Earth with it.

The question is: How fast can we achieve critical mass in raising the vibration of light through the light workers? We have a short time in order to catch up to the rest of our systems. We have a short time in order to catch up with the wishes and the desires of our planet Mother Earth.

Many of the dimensions of reality that have been experienced in linear time on your planet have already folded upon themselves or joined the light. One dimension of reality which is lagging behind is yours, the one that you are experiencing, your physical reality.

The forces of light that are held within the realm of the ascended masters and mistresses of light are doing everything in their power to assist you, to hold you in a tunnel of light, to create a vacuum of light around you for the changes that are imminent and for the beams of light that are about to hit your planet to be filtered in order not to burn you out.

Many of the masters and mistresses of light come through light workers such as yourself, channeling light, channeling healing, channeling wisdom, channeling higher vibrations, channeling light energies, anchoring light vibrations. All of this is happening with great force, hope, joy, celebration.

I want to see you join us in this celebration.

I want to be the father, the mother that has the joy of seeing my children graduate in light.

I want to celebrate your glory on your return journey to light.

I bring you this discourse to remind you that
it is your divine right to be returned to the light,
light of its purest and brightest essence.

Rise, my children, join me. Run to me. Give me permission to assist you. Call upon me. Call upon the Sisterhoods and Brotherhoods of Melchizedek and Lady Melchai. Join the ascended masters and mistresses of light.

Will yourself to attain the mastery necessary to make you attain the merit of rubbing shoulders with ascended masters and mistresses of light.

Will yourself to be light.
Will yourself to love light, to choose light.
Will yourself to bring light to Earth.

Decree this light to be penetrated through all the kingdoms for which you have been given the guardianship.

You, my beloved children
who are light workers, are our only hope.

You are the light in my eyes. You are the beams of light that shine forth from the heart of the cosmic Sun, the Undifferentiated Source, in the heart core of our cosmos. You are the ones who have been called to service.

Heed our call. Serve the light. Awaken other souls. Come to the rescue. Relieve the three kingdoms of all darkness and dross. Let go of pain and suffering.

Surrender to the light. Obey the light. Serve the light. Love the light. Become the light. Shine the light. Be the antenna. Transmit the light. Transmute darkness.

Relieve your planet from darkness.
Hold her up to the light.

Send her to where she belongs amongst her brothers and sisters in light. And through that, you will give her the opportunity to ascend and move in the light and you will give your own brothers and sisters, the masses, humankind the opportunity to awaken to the light.

You yourselves will be rewarded a thousand fold, a million fold. You will be rewarded from eternity to eternity.

May the light bless you from eternity to eternity. I am your father Melchizedek.

Lakshmi

I first learned about Lakshmi when I saw her picture in an ashram in upstate New York. She was standing in the center of a lotus, holding a book in one of her six hands. The picture was in front of an altar on which sat various objects, including a box with a slot meant for financial donations.

As I stared at this picture, the goddess came alive. She told me to give her all the money in my purse and in return, she would give me ten times as much as I gave her.

I got the idea that this was a test and one I obviously had to pass in order to get to the next level. I needed to learn to trust this goddess before she could shower me with her blessings.

It was not an easy decision for me. If I gave all the money I had, I would have nothing for the five and a half hour drive I faced to get back home to Massachusetts. It was a long time to be without any cash. So it was with some trepidation that I gave the goddess all the money in my wallet.

When I got home, there was a check waiting for me that was much more than ten times as much money that I had given Lakshmi. The money was owed to me but I had thought that I would never get it.

Lakshmi is revered by all Hindus. Melchizedek, who I channeled on the eve of the Hindu Festival of Lights in 1997, offered some thoughts on Lakshmi and the rest of us...

Comments on Lakshmi from Melchizedek

Channeled October 28, 1997

I am Melchizedek... We are on the brink of the festival of Diwali. Diwali is the Festival of Lights, the festival during which all of India celebrates and honors the Goddess.

The Goddess is known in India as Goddess Lakshmi. Lakshmi is the bringer of good fortune, both spiritual fortune as well as material fortune. In many pictures of Lakshmi, you see that she is depicted to be holding the book of knowledge in one hand, offering spiritual knowledge with another hand, and showering golden coins with another hand.

The Indian New Year begins on the day after the festival of Diwali...

I ask those of you who have not had an experience of Goddess Lakshmi to prepare yourself for a gift, for a boon, for this goddess is extremely generous by nature and extremely loving as well. In her love for humanity, she has offered to help and align the will of humanity with the will of God.

For this reason, you see in her pictures that she is depicted as having four, six, eight, or a thousand arms. She is offering her assistance to humanity. And she is lending more than one hand; she is offering a thousand helping hands to humanity.

It is also interesting to note that Lakshmi is the golden aspect of Quan Yin. That means that the two are one. In both the Chinese and the Indian culture, each represents the goddess energy. In the Orient, China, Japan, and Tibet, Quan Yin holds the mother energy; she is the bringer of boons and has the energy of love within her. In India, it is Goddess Lakshmi who is loved, who is held with honor and respect in every home, in every temple.

It is Lakshmi to whom people in India make offerings daily, in the same way that people in China and Japan make offerings to Quan Yin daily. Prayers begin with adorning Lakshmi with flowers and the day ends with adorning Lakshmi with prayers of thanksgiving and blessing.

Would you not call this a universally auspicious day, when the entire world honors, respects and blesses the God within each other, the Goddess within each other, the Goddess in each home and in each heart?

Would it be any different, do you think, when people begin every day with the name of God and end the day in the name of God? It wouldn't matter whether this is the male aspect of God, the female aspect of God, or the child aspect of God, or even the formless aspect of God that is honored at least twice a day.

I am with you for that hope. I await that day that happens with great hope. I wish and I pray and I also ask that each one of you who reads these words and who becomes acquainted with various means of extending love to God and receiving love from God, start practicing these methods if you have not already done so.

I ask that you offer each day to God or to whatever supreme consciousness you believe in, whether it is God or Source or Goddess or child, or even your spouse; in what ever shape or form you love, extend love from your heart to that supreme consciousness. If it is Great Spirit, start each day by offering the day to the Great Spirit, and end each day by offering the day to the Great Spirit.

Eat each meal, offering the meal to the Great Spirit; start each job offering the job to the Great Spirit; take your shower offering the water to the Great Spirit, offer the cleansing of your body to Great Spirit; ask that Great Spirit cleanse your spiritual body as the water cleanses your physical body.

Offer each word before it is spoken to Great Spirit; offer each action before it is performed to Great Spirit; offer each thought before you act on it to the Great Spirit.

Live each day in this way and you will see that your entire life will change. Life will become joyful, love will pour into your being, love will lead you where you need to go, decisions will be made for you the simplest way.

Once you have aligned your will with the will of God by offering all that you do to God, you will know what you need to do. Whether you worship the Great Spirit, Source, All That Is, Goddess, Self Within, once the offering is made, all is well.

We make this prayer in the wish and in the hope that the day will come when we all do this as part of our daily routine, when this becomes as involuntary as breathing.

I cheer you on and bless you for that day.

In hope and in anticipation, I am Melchizedek.

Eight Gifts from the Goddess of Fortune

Commentary: Although this was channeled at the time of Diwali in 1997, we have been guided to include it here to make the gifts and the energies of Lakshmi available to all. You can easily reconnect to the energy of the Goddess by merely reading these words. After you have read this through once on a purely intellectual level and you wish to receive what Lakshmi offers, make this your intention and read the Goddess's words again, this time from your heart.

Lakshmi, channeled October 28, 1997

My children of light, I am Lakshmi. My Beloved Lord Melchizedek has given me a cheery introduction. I pray I make good on his promises.

It is true that the festival of Diwali in India is in honor and celebration of Goddess Lakshmi, and it is also true that Lakshmi brings your wishes and desires. For that purpose, I am here to present myself to you so that we may both benefit from each other's company.

In this auspicious time of the year, while in many continents you are experiencing coldness and a process of hibernation, we in India celebrate the Festival of Lights. These lights shine not only upon India, but they shine throughout the entire universe. It is the victory of light, it is the joy of light, it is the union of light with love that we celebrate.

It is not only celebrated on one continent; it is an offering to the entire world. There is no need for any particular area of the world to be treated differently from others.

When it is time for festivities, would it not be wonderful if the whole world participated in the love and light together? It is to that end that I have come to offer and grant you a wish or two; and I might add that this entire book is full of wish fulfilling energies that all the deities and masters are bringing to you. It is a great honor and pleasure to be included in this wondrous group of beings.

I now ask that you close your eyes and focus your attention on your third eye. As you enter the divine space of the third eye, you see a blue pearl, and the blue pearl is small and shiny like a star, and as you watch it, the blue pearl comes closer and closer to you.

As it stands before you, it feels as if it is absorbing you to itself. You find yourself suddenly inside the blue pearl, and even though you are inside a small pearl, the space around you is larger than a stadium, but it looks more like some kind of palace, and everything has a golden-blue color to it.

Standing in the middle is Goddess Lakshmi wearing all of her golden ornaments. She wears a crown of gold on her head, and she has eight arms, which is the universal number for luck and good fortune.

In your vision of her, she holds a lotus, the first flower that was brought upon this planet Earth. The lotus is the flower of wisdom, the flower of the gods and goddesses.

In her second hand she holds a conch shell. The wisdom of the seas is blown through the conch, and the wisdom of the seas held within the energy of the conch shell is also a gift that Lakshmi brings. When a conch is blown, the sound heard is the manifestation of the wisdom of the beings of the sea.

In her third hand Lakshmi holds the book of knowledge, the book of wisdom. This book is from higher levels and dimensions and can only be read with the inner vision once the third eye is opened. When this book is open, pure golden white light pours out of it. This golden white light is all-seeing, all-knowing. It is omnipotent, omniscient and omnipresent. This is the book of knowledge that Lakshmi offers to you.

In her fourth hand Lakshmi holds the discus, which is a disc with jagged razor edges, and with this, Lakshmi destroys the ego and releases the karma of whoever prays to her for release. She throws the discus like a boomerang, and as the disc cuts through your ego, she transmutes all karmic attachment into the ethers. This is her fourth gift to you.

From her fifth hand Lakshmi showers great quantities of gold coins, the sign and the symbol for material fortune that Lakshmi brings to you.

In her sixth hand Lakshmi holds a golden globe, which is a sign for material abundance. The golden globe holds within it the material abundance, which you desire.

The golden globe is also a sign and symbol for manifesting that which you desire from higher realms and dimensions into the third dimension of existence. This golden globe and the manifestation of your desires is another gift that is given to you.

In her seventh hand Lakshmi holds a jar of dew, a jar of the clearest water that can be brought from the heavens down to Earth. On top of the jar that holds the purest waters of heavens is a coconut, which is the offering that is given to the gods for the removal of obstacles.

By bringing you the purest and clearest waters from the heavens down to Earth, Lakshmi washes and cleanses your karma and purifies your destiny.

By holding the coconut, she is offering on your behalf that all obstacles be removed from your path of sadhana, your path of spiritual practices, your path of aligning your will with the will of God.

Lakshmi holds her eighth hand with the palm facing you. This is the sign of peace, the sign of prosperity, the sign of harmony and love. This is the exchange of love from the hand of Lakshmi to the heart of all of you.

With this mudra [a hand gesture] Lakshmi offers from her heart healing, health, wholeness and love through her hand into the being, the heart, the body and the third eye of her devotees. Anyone who receives from this hand of Lakshmi becomes whole again, remembers unity, remembers union of the one with The One, as one. All is love, and love is all, and The One is love.

As she stands before you, Goddess Lakshmi offers to you in this auspicious moment these eight gifts. Take a deep breath and as you breathe deeply, think of one, two, or three other spiritual or non-spiritual desires that you have.

Imagine that whenever you read this book, it is a new life, a new beginning, a rebirthing. Even if you read these words over and over, consider each time you read them to be a new birth and a new beginning.

With that in mind, ask and I shall bring to you the object of your desires. Make a wish or two or three. Go in your heart and ask it, "O beloved heart, what is it that you desire? What shall I ask Goddess Lakshmi to bring in this auspicious time of the Festival of Lights for me, for my rebirthing, for my renewal, for my recreation?"

Let your heart rule your mind. Let your heart tell the mind that which it desires, and when the desire enters your heart, deliver your wish to Lakshmi.

Tell Lakshmi, "O Goddess, I desire..." and specifically mention your desire, and allow me to take that prayer to the One Great Spirit, to the Source of All That Is, to the Supreme Consciousness. Allow me to pray on your behalf, allow me to intercede on your behalf for the fulfillment of your desires.

This is my gift to you in thanksgiving for the introduction that my Lord Melchizedek has given to me. I am always as your Mother. As the Divine Mother has said, every goddess holds the love of the child within her heart, and I hold the love within my heart any time you desire to speak to me.

Call upon Lakshmi any time you desire to express a wish. Speak to me, ask for Lakshmi any time you feel sad, call upon Lakshmi any time you need help, call upon Lakshmi. Any time you feel you are stuck, whether it is with material prosperity or spiritual prosperity, call upon Lakshmi. Any time you desire further abundance in your life, call upon Lakshmi. Lakshmi is here, at your service.

Lakshmi I AM, I AM, I AM.

And so it is.

Meditate on yourself.
Worship yourself. Love yourself.
God dwells within you as you.

- Swami Muktananda, a saint from India who died in 1982

Michael

In literature and traditions from around the world— Christian, Jewish and Islamic— Archangel Michael is one of the greatest of the angels. In the Torah, he comes as the chief of the angels and he is the precursor to the Messiah. In the Arabic of the Qur'an, he is Mikal— *Whoever is an enemy to Allah and his angels and prophets, to Gabriel and Michael— Lo! Allah is an enemy to those who reject faith.* (Surah of The Cow, 1:98)

In Exodus in the Bible, the Lord warns that he is sending an angel— *Beware of him and obey his voice; do not provoke him, for he will not pardon your transgressions; for my name is in him.* (Exodus 23:20-21) In Hebrew the name Michael— Mikael — means *with God* or *who is God.*

The fifth century Persian saint-poet Nasar Khosro says Archangel Michael is the guardian of wisdom and knowledge. The sixth century Persian saint-poet Khaghani says Michael is "the secret holder of abundance... Don't do with less when Michael is at hand."

According to Islamic tradition, Michael is one of the four angels around the Throne of God. (The others are Gabriel, Azriel and Raphael.) It is understood that the angels that come on the Night of Power during Ramadan, the holy month of fasting, are Michael and Gabriel. As the Qur'an says, *The Night of Power is better than a thousand months, therein the Angels and the Spirit by their Lord's decree, leave and come down. That night is peace till break of dawn.* (97:1-5)

Bashtar was an ancient Persian name for Archangel Michael. During the Sassanian period (226-641 AD) there was a race who called themselves Mikaelian, meaning *of Michael* (Mikael) or *descendants of Michael*, according to *A Persian Dictionary*, by

Dr. Mohammad Mo'in (University of Tehran). These Mikaelians were said to have brought wealth, light, abundance, wisdom and honor.

Archangel Michael has told me that he and his legions of angels have taken human form on Earth to rescue humankind from the misery of duality and separation from God. We need rescuing because we have forgotten that we are divine and a part of God.

Michael is the keeper of the Sword of Mercy. Part of his mission is healing. For him to rescue us, we need to be healed, to be brought to wholeness. He and his consort or partner Lady Faith are guardian angels of the First Ray, the blue ray of divine will.

By the year 2005, Michael says, he will begin rebuilding our Earth with threads of gold, silver and platinum. That year will mark the beginning of a seven-year cycle of prosperity and this will be the driving force that ushers in a new golden age.

As a girl, I read the Farsi translation of the Qu'ran and the Hadith, the sayings of the Prophet Muhammad, so I was familiar with the energy of Michael. When I prayed, I would see Michael standing in front of me. I also was very aware of a pillar of light that he always held in his hand. Many years later when I began to channel, I learned that this light was Michael's Sword of Mercy. The image of Michael I saw and still see today is the same image I saw as a girl when I lived in Iran.

The Blue Flame of Divine Love

Michael, channeled May 14, 2003

We bring you gifts of light, gifts of empowerment, gifts of power, gifts of mercy, gifts of love, and the greatest gift of all, the gift of clearing your pathway so you can return to the heart of the Undifferentiated Source where you truly belong.

My brethren of light, I am Michael. In the presence of my beloved loving consort Lady Faith, I stand with my Sword of Mercy above your heads and I offer to each one of you the Blue Flame of Divine Love to open your hearts and to reawaken you to your own true divine nature.

We come from the legions and hosts of the angels and archangels, the realms of the angelic beings. We have made a sacrifice of our time and our life in service to God for the benefit of humankind.

We stand ready to offer our guidance and our help, clearing and cleansing the path of light before you so that you can walk stepping into light, seeing as you walk in the direction of your return journey to the heart of God.

We clear your pathway with great joy. We offer you light from the heart of the Undifferentiated Source through the Blue Flame. We offer you assistance by annihilating all darkness around you, by holding the Sword of Mercy above your head.

The Sword of Mercy, taken out, ready to transmute all dross, all negativity and all darkness, is a sign to the entire manifested universe that this is the final step on the path of the return journey home. This is a sign to express to all who care to hear that we are at your service, as we are in the service of the light.

Through the guidance of the light, through the mercy that has been bestowed upon us with the Sword of Mercy, the power that has been bestowed upon us through the Scepter of Power, the crown that has been bestowed upon us, the Crown of Glory, the cape that has been bestowed upon us, the Cape of Empowerment, we bring you gifts of light, gifts of empowerment, gifts of power, gifts of mercy, gifts of love, and the greatest gift of all, the gift of clearing your pathway so you can return to the heart of the Undifferentiated Source where you truly belong.

This is your divine right and we, the legions of Michael and Faith, have offered to stand guard over you, the divine human beings, to assist you on your path of return journey home.

Heed our assistance. Call upon us. Say this prayer and we will be your guiding light:

Prayer for the Guiding Light

I call upon Archangel Michael and Lady Faith to come forth and be my guiding light, bringing the Sword of Mercy and blazing the sword above my head.

Archangel Michael above me.

Archangel Michael below me.

Archangel Michael in front of me.

Archangel Michael behind me.

Archangel Michael to my right.

Archangel Michael to my left.

Archangel Michael, guide me on the path of light on the return journey home.

Archangel Michael, protect me from all harm, from all darkness and bring me to light.

Archangel Michael, guide me, protect me, bring me power, mercy, glory, light. Bring me back to the heart of my Father-Mother God-self. Bring me to my divine heritage. Bring me home in the light.

I stand loving and protecting you in the presence of the legions of Michael, in the presence of the legions of the cosmic light, the cosmic beings of light, the ascended masters of light, the masters and mistresses of light, the brotherhoods and sisterhoods of light.

Let light blaze forth! Let light blaze forth! Let light blaze forth!

In love and light, I am your brother Michael.

Activating the Sword of Mercy

Commentary: This is a meditation to re-ignite the Sword of Mercy that each of us has embodied as light energy in our spines. This sword is actually a pillar of light that resembles the blue sword of light used by Luke Skywalker in the Star Wars movies.

For most of us, our Sword of Mercy is not illuminated. When Archangel Michael activates it, it begins to shine a blue light. The sword is a tool to use to return to God unity, to use just as Michael uses his Sword of Mercy— to battle the darkness and all it contains (including, for instance, sickness, fear, and other negativity).

An illumined Sword of Mercy is also a declaration, an unmistakable signal to all worlds, including the lower forces (such as those in Hell and the Underworld and the disembodied souls in the astral or psychic realm), that this soul is of the light. Archangel Michael has the power to illuminate our individual Sword of Mercy with his own sword upon our asking. Remember that he cannot interfere with our free will. This process cannot be done for us unless we ask for it.

Read Michael's words through once and, if you wish to participate, prepare yourself for meditation. Sit comfortably, take a few deep breaths and read this again, visualizing the images and issuing the decrees, as he instructs.

Michael, channeled May 31, 2003

My brethren of light, I am Michael. I bless you with my heart and my soul. I thank you for presenting your love and light, and I thank you for this communion. I offer to you a recalibration of the Sword of Mercy, and activation of illumination of the light upon your physical spinal column.

If you wish to give me permission to perform this activation and recalibration, please say that you do.

Once you have given me permission for this activation and recalibration, you will energetically receive from me a rod of light in the color of fluorescent aqua marine blue. It is placed from the base of your spine five inches below your tail bone as a rod of light moving all the way up to the top of your head five inches above your crown chakra.

If you wish me to proceed with this process, say:

Yes, Archangel Michael, in the name of the I AM That I AM, I ask that you proceed with the light of this activation.

Take a deep breath, close your eyes and pause for a moment as the activation takes place.

You may be feeling a tingling sensation in your body, most especially in your hands. This is due to the recalibration of the Rod of Mercy, the Sword of Mercy.

The time has come for humankind to receive this illumination and as you receive this illuminated light, you become the beacons of light that will anchor its energy through the heart core of Mother Earth and through the web of light, the grid system of your individual bodies as well as the grid system of the planet.

The process is complete. I bless you, I love you, I hold you in my heart and I will do everything in my power to illuminate this light within you, whatever is in your highest interest and according to the light of the I AM.

Activating the Crown of Glory

Commentary: In this meditation, Michael offers the Crown of Glory, a tool for reconnecting our higher chakras or energy centers to that of the Godhead, which is to say God, the source of all that is. When the crown of glory is in place on your head, it connects— via our silver cord, which is our soul connection— to the pure white light in the heart core of God. Then, a pillar of light descends upon us from the heavens above, forming a cylinder of light that totally encircles our bodies. This pillar of light raises our vibration to that of the divine beings that we are, and facilitates our connection with the presence of the I AM in the heavenly realms and the spark of the I AM within our own hearts.

Michael, channeled May 31, 2003

My brethren of light, I am Michael. I offer you the Crown of Glory. This crown is a catalyst for your connection with your own source of light, a re-connection with the Godhead.

When you wear this crown, it encapsulates your crown chakra on the top of your head, and it sits right over your third eye. It also creates of band of light around your head.

Sometimes after working with light (and this may include intense prayer and meditations), you feel pain in your head and you wonder why. Sometimes you feel the pain like a band of light right around your head and on top. Sometimes you may have felt like the top of your head is exploding. You might feel pain because of the intensity of light when the energy is being poured down into you.

[This light is expanding inside your head and reactivating your pituitary and pineal glands so that you can receive more light. The intensity of the expanding light almost always causes a headache. If this pain becomes difficult for you to bear, call on Archangel Michael and ask him to relieve you of this pain. Remember that in this world of free will, our guides cannot even take our pain away unless we ask for this assistance.]

The offering of the Crown of Glory, the Crown of Mercy, the Crown of Power is the reconnection of those higher chakras of your body to the chakras of the Godhead, the Universal Mind, the Universal Heart.

This crown is made of solid 24 carat gold. Gold is the highest energy metal available on Earth. The presence of gold is to transmute negativity and raise the vibration of everything and all life.

In times of prosperity, in times of high spirituality, veins of gold come to the surface of Earth and are used by people of each civilization to raise their own consciousness to attain greater spiritual awakening and growth.

In times of confusion, veins of gold recede deeper and deeper into the heart core of Mother Earth because in the wrong hands, it will either have to stay dormant or the chaos will magnify itself.

Gold is a very high consciousness being of light. When you receive the Crown of Gold, the gold itself is your best friend. The gold provides an encapsulated cylinder of light. It protects, re-vibrates, refreshes and revitalizes your most important spiritual chakras— your crown, your third eye (in the middle of your forehead).

On the top of the crown, there is a gem. You may be receiving one of seven different gems on your own Crown of Glory. It could be a ruby, an emerald, blue sapphire, diamond, opal, orange sapphire or pearl. These gems represent the qualities of the Seven Rays.

Once you're fully connected to the energy-wide vibration of the godhead, you will benefit from the qualities of all the seven gems connecting you to the seven rays of creation. This in turn reconnects you to the Seven Mighty Elohim, the cosmic beings of light, who are guardians of the Seven Rays.

My promise to you is that your lives will change for the better with this crown. You may see chaos and confusion around you but you will be in your peace and harmony; you will be in your own love and light. My promise to you is that I will continue to encapsulate you in light.

I offer you now the Crown of Glory, a golden crown. Take a deep breath and feel the presence of the crown on your head.

See yourself standing in a pillar of pure white light and say:

I call upon the pillar of light from the heart of the I AM That I AM to create a cylinder of light around me, illuminating my body and being.

Prayer for a Shower of Blue Light

Commentary: In this exercise, Archangel Michael and Lady Faith and their legions give you a shower of blue light, which will continue to pour upon you energetically every hour, half hour and quarter hour for as long as you wish to receive it. Use it in good faith and good fellowship and in service to the light and Mother Earth.

This shower of blue light will cover you like a blanket and bring you protection from all harm. In time, as you grow spiritually and evolve on your path of service, an energetic blue cape will form around you, surrounding you with the protection of the legions of Michael and Lady Faith. In time, you will recognize this energy as the Blue Cape of Empowerment. Some among you who have already begun on your path of service with the legions of Michael and Faith are already empowered with the blue cape and carry it around you energetically and etherically at all times. When you finish this exercise, take a deep breath and be still for as long as you need to be.

Michael, channeled May 31, 2003

My brethren of light, I am Michael. I offer a prayer and, if you wish to receive it, I set it in motion so that you receive this help every hour on the hour, on the half hour, on the quarter hour— a shower of blue light from the heart core of the legions of Michael, to protect you, bless you, to empower you, to bring you success and most importantly to bring you spiritual growth and prosperity. Expect the best for yourselves. You have taken a human form in these troubled times of Earth's evolution. Why should you not have prosperity? Why should you not have the best of all good things available? Demand it of the universe. It is owed to you. We cannot give it unless you ask, so start asking.

Start praying. Tell the Universe in its glory:

I call upon the forces of light in the universe.

In the name of the I AM That I AM, I ask the universe to:

Give me what is owed to me in goodness and in light.

Bring me the prosperity, the comfort and the luxury that will assist me in offering my services to light.

Take away the pain of the mundane subsistence living. I should not struggle for my livelihood.

I AM a powerful being of light.

I AM here to serve.

I AM a beacon of light.

I AM holding the original blueprint in my heart.

Make me abundant.

Open the doors of abundance and prosperity.

Give me the power to know what to do with it.

Give me the power to only serve the light with the prosperity and abundance.

Holding the Light

Michael, channeled May 31, 2003

Love your teachers and pray for them. Love your government officials even when you do not agree with them. Send them love.

My brethren of light, I am Michael. Call upon me. I am here at your service. I am your humble servant. I have come to rescue the Earth.

You are my helpers. You hold your hands out and your hands become my hands. You see through your eyes and your eyes become my eyes. I see through your eyes, I speak through your mouth, I touch through your hands, I walk through your feet. Give me a chance to guide you and assist you, to walk before you and protect you.

When you sit in your car, call upon me to place a shield of light around your car to protect your car while you are driving. When you get to your work places, call upon me to place a bubble of light around you, around everyone, around the entire building. When you go home, call upon me to create a bubble of light around your house. All this will only take a split second; you just connect to the light in a split second.

You don't have to check to see if you are breathing; you know you are breathing. In the same way, when you call to my presence, I am there as long as you breathe and as long as you wish me to help you.

Once in a while check to see if you have the seven aspects of Michael above you, below you, in front, behind you, to your left, your right and in your heart.

Before you leave your house, call upon me to stand with my Sword of Mercy above my head in the house until you come back so that no harm in the form of energy or in the form of human trespassing would ever come to your homes, to your hearts, to your workplaces, to your children, to your loved ones, to those who have been given into your hands and in your guardianships.

Love your teachers and pray for them. Love your government officials even when you do not agree with them. Send them love. Constantly and continuously send Archangel Michael and his legions to clear and purify them of their dross so that they can make all the decisions right for the Light.

There is only one right decision, the decision that is made to further the light, to expand the light, to contain the light, to receive the light. And all of it can be done with the one invocation: Michael, blaze forth the Light!

See yourself in a cylinder of light. See your Sword of Mercy illuminated. See your crown of gold pulsating. See the sphere in your heart spinning.

Do this daily as part of your daily routine. After awhile, it will be part of your being. You don't have to think it; you just remember it.

Check to see if you have a cylinder of light around you, if you are in the light, in the presence of the pure white light of the I AM That I AM. Once in a while check and see that the Sword of Mercy continues to illuminate and vibrate the blue light.

Do this for the light. As light beings, you can hold the vibration until we can take the Earth into the next phase.

The ascended masters— with their thought forms, with their pure white light thoughts reflected upon the globe— have created a bubble of light around the Earth; so that as your Earth is shifting, as the poles are shifting, you will simply just see it as floods, earthquakes, volcanoes, simple weather changes.

Those who are unaware will continue to remain unaware that we are shifting the poles, we are moving our orbit, we are closing this phase. We are moving into the new rebirthing of Earth as a star. The seventh Golden Age, the Age of Knowledge— the Mayans call it the Age of Itza. The emblem of this age is the eagle.

I hope, I pray, and I ask for the light to shine upon Earth. I ask you for your prayers so that we can succeed to the highest light above and beyond any limitation. What we put into the grid of the Earth now will decide the future of the new Earth, the ascended Earth. The more light we can bring together, the higher the vibration we can attain when we move into this new cycle.

I hold you all in my heart. With great love, with great joy, I stand at your feet. I am your brother Michael.

And so it is.

Merging with the I AM That I AM

Michael, channeled May 31, 2003

My brethren of light, I am Michael. You may remain in love and light, but remember that the atmosphere of your planet is filled with energies that wish for you to not succeed. The reason for this is that it is their job to test you. That is the greater reason. You grow and become more worthy of greater light when you pass these tests.

From their point of view, they are lost in the task they are here to perform. They chose to serve humanity by distracting humankind from the light that is their divine right and through the distraction, teach humanity a lesson. In the process, they forgot that they themselves belong to God as well.

So, in the fear of God, in the fear of being punished by God, they hide away from the light. And yet because they know that light is their divine right and their only way back to freedom, they are attracted to light.

The more light that you raise, the more the possibility of these beings coming to see what you are up to. In the process of them seeing what you have been up to, it's like an egg that has gone bad. It smells like sulfur, like a skunk that has gone into fear and has thrown its skunky smells. You may not smell the smells, you may not taste the taste, but it is there.

How it manifests is in setting you back. How it manifests is by creating chaos and confusion. How it manifests is that you forget what you were going to do. How it manifests is that you make a phone call and someone very unhelpful pulls you down from that high of the pure white light where you started from.

You can be disrespectful and hurtful or you can just cut yourself off and say a prayer of blessing and be done with that conversation and start all over again. The next move before you start over again would be to say this:

I call upon the luminous magical presence of the I AM That I AM.

You don't have to say those adjectives, just call upon the I AM That I AM. There will come a time when you want to give 10 adjectives— luminous, victorious, glorious.

So, begin by calling upon the presence of the I AM That I AM. Ask that the presence of the I AM That I AM join and merge with you.

If you have difficulty feeling a change or a shift in your own energy field, then it is important that you ask for the tunnel of light to surround you.

Sometimes your vibration can move to such a low level that the presence of the I AM That I AM cannot reach you. There is a certain level below which the I AM energies will not reach. You have to raise your vibration. If you are in such a situation, then ask for the tunnel of light, cylinder of light, pillar of light, however you say it is fine.

Once you feel the presence of the I AM That I AM, invoke it and believe that it is there. Make your heart convince the mind that it is there.

Say:

I call upon my heart, my spirit, my soul and my mind to raise their vibrations upwards through my crown chakra inside the pillar of light.

I move to higher light from my crown chakra to reach to the presence of the I AM That I AM.

Start moving up. Move your energy upward. Move your heart, your spirit, your soul and your mind upward through your crown chakra inside this pillar of light in the direction of higher light above your crown chakra to reach to your presence of the I AM That I AM.

Merge with the Presence and ask that the Presence merge into you through your crown chakra, down into your body.

Feel the Presence all the way down to the tips of your toes. Feel the Presence extend down to the core of the Earth.

Intend that this protection will continue for the next 24 or 48 hours. [Michael offers this protection to last for up to 48 hours every time you invoke his name and ask for it.]

Wherever you meet the luminous, magical, mighty, victorious, glorious Presence, absorb, digest, merge, unite with it. When you have completed the merging, then bring down the merged essence of light to yourself, returning your heart, your mind, your spirit, your soul back into your body.

If you feel that you would like to get a much higher boost, do this process three times.

If you are in the middle of a telephone conversation or in the middle of a business day and you just want to boost yourself, make sure that on the third attempt that you and your luminous Presence come back into your body.

If you are in meditation and you wish to receive an answer, on the third attempt— after you have blessed your physical body twice and you have brought the energy down to the recesses of your finger tips, your toes and from the bottom of your feet to the core of Mother Earth— on the third attempt, you may go up and stay there and receive guidance.

Each time you practice this, the energy will take you to a higher level. Instead of the Presence lowering itself, the Presence will take you to the higher level and will then come back down with you into your body.

In the first round you meet and you merge and unite. Intend to bring back the Presence and imbue your body from the top of your head all the way to the bottom of your feet, all the way to the core of Mother Earth.

Then you start round two, your heart, soul, spirit and mind moving up again inside the pillar of white light into the presence of the I AM That I AM, mixing, merging and uniting in oneness.

Pull that energy vibration into your crown chakra, into every chakra of your body down to the bottom of your feet and from your feet into the core of Mother Earth.

The third time, go back up the same way, even higher. This time, after you have merged with the I AM Presence, you ask your questions.

You can directly ask the presence of the I AM That I AM. And you can choose to ask for the presence of whatever masters and mistresses of light, angels, archangels, seraphim, cherubim, guides, and guardian angels you wish. Feel their energy and in the presence of the I AM That I AM, ask the questions you would like to put to them. Invoke myself and the presence of my legions, by all means. I am here at your service.

When you are complete with your questions, just so you can replenish your body as you are coming down, bring forth the united and merged essence of the I AM That I AM down into your body.

You may do this exercise because you feel you are being attacked or you feel you are taking a down turn, because you feel you need an energy boost, because you feel you need to shift and change the energy, because you feel something is not right in the atmosphere, because things are not moving in a positive direction.

Even if you are in the middle of a meeting, even if you are in the middle of a group conversation, even if you are with a client, a patient, a child, and you feel as though your words are not penetrating, you feel as though you are losing your focus, excuse yourself for a moment and go into the restroom. These are times when you can have a precious moment of aloneness to regroup.

It will take you perhaps two minutes at first. As you do this, it becomes instantaneous. Pull your energy all the way up, meet and merge with the presence of the I AM That I AM, bring the energy all the way down, take it to the core of Mother Earth. Start from the heart again— the heart, the spirit, the soul and the mind— moving up again through the crown chakra, meeting and merging with the presence of the I AM That I AM.

The presence of the I AM That I AM is your divine right. The presence of the I AM That I AM is the essence of the being that will return you to oneness. The ultimate journey of oneness is through this presence.

Joan of Arc: My friends. This sword has come to us from God. It is his sign that we are right and we shall win. But be not over-awed. And let your hearts beat softly in its light. He means to show, however small you are, however weak, when you will find his light, and stand within, your power will grow and blend with his.

- from Karen Sunde's play *Me and Joan*

Elohim Hercules

Elohim Hercules is one of the Seven Mighty Elohim or Seven Builders of Creation. They are the guardians of the cosmic powers that created this planet and brought the powers of Nature upon it for our use.

The Elohim are also called the Seven Powers Around the Throne and Seven Builders Around the Throne, mentioned in the Bible— *There in Heaven stood a throne, and on the throne sat one whose appearance was like the gleam of jasper and carnelian... Burning before the throne were seven flaming torches, the seven spirits of God.* (Revelation 4:2-5)

The Elohim are concerned with manifestation in this physical world— within our physical bodies, our minds, our feelings and the atmosphere around us.

They project the Sevenfold Flame through our brains within our foreheads to empower us to connect with the divine mind of God and the cosmic beings of light, and to protect against the misuse of the powers of the mind. Each of the Seven Elohim's heart flames makes up the Sevenfold Flame, which— once re-ignited— is an extension of their life in us. They say the Sevenfold Flame is multidimensional energy that will take us back to our oneness in the heart core of God.

Elohim is the Hebrew word for gods; the singular is eloha. However, in the Bible, Elohim is often used in the singular as one of the words for God. Hercules refers to herself or himself as Elohim Hercules.

The Elohim say they are about 15 feet tall. Each has a masculine and a feminine aspect. The feminine aspect of Hercules is called Amazon. The primary quality of this Elohim is power and strength, attained through love.

I knew nothing about the Elohim until another ascended being, Metatron, first discussed them with me about five years ago. Metatron said the Elohim were "great beings of this universe." First he introduced me to the collective essence of the Elohim during group channelings. Then he said that as I channeled him, he would bring the Elohim in, one by one, so that I and the others present could become acquainted with their energies.

Metatron called the Elohim by their qualities— power, peace, abundance, truth, and such. All of the Elohim share the same qualities but one is predominate in each.

Metatron also said these beings lived in a realm of semi-form, which means that their quotient of light is so high, that we all-form humans have to raise our vibration to commune with them. (Archangel Michael gives us an exercise to do this in his discourse about the Merging with the I AM Presence.)

As I prepared to begin channeling, with Victoria at my side in the summer of 2003, Elohim Hercules came through. Victoria and I were putting together material for this book, as we had been divinely instructed to do. But until this moment, no Elohim had weighed in on this project. I was quite surprised to hear: *Beloveds, I am Hercules. Bear with me as I adjust to the energies in your realm of reality.*

The energies of Elohim Hercules were nothing like the kind of masculine energy of this Elohim's namesake, who is Hercules (Herakles in Greek), the strongest and biggest man alive, according to the Greek myths. But the energy, the voice, the entire presence of Elohim Hercules was decidedly gentle and almost feminine.

Remembering Your True Origin

Elohim Hercules, channeled July 11, 2003

What good is this breath that you take if it does not lead you to the divinity that is waiting for you...? What good is this life if you live it unconscious of your own divinity?

The time has come for the vibrations of the Seven Mighty Elohim to be lowered to the atmosphere of Earth and to be received by the hearts and souls of those willing and accepting of these energies, even though small in number. The velocity and intensity of these vibrations that we emanate will lead you to the completion of this task. We will make up for the smallness of the numbers with our purity of light and intensity of light. In order for you to receive the light that will emanate upon you, you must in turn receive and accept purity and intensity within yourself.

This means that whatever is of mistrusting and other negative energies— such as betrayal, judgment, greed, deception, cheating, lying— has to be released and replaced by purity of intent and returned to their original innocence intended for all divine beings of light.

It also means that the intensity of light that is emanated to you is of greater nature. Therefore, this light upon contact with impurities will burn. This burning sensation you will experience within yourself as the thoughts that burn your mind, as the emotions that feel like burning your emotional body, as sicknesses that burn your physical body.

I use the analogy of burning to make the point— burning is one way to purify and to return to the original intent.

Therefore, if lately you have been feeling the burden of life becoming more difficult and your daily chores more difficult to bear, know that it is because your own body, spirit, mind and soul is being purified and cleansed in the fire of ascension, in the flame of the ascension and that there is a purpose and a reason for what you are experiencing and suffering from.

The reason is that your bodies, minds, emotions, spirits and souls are being accelerated to the point of receiving greater light and being purified at that accelerated pace in order to assist you and make you beacons of light who assist the rest of the souls and the planet to make the final leap into its ascension.

Make your grid of light at this time. Consider it as important as the food that you eat on a daily basis, as the bathing that you need on a daily basis, as the breath that you take.

What good is this breath that you take if it does not lead you to the divinity that is waiting for you to embrace it? What good is this life if you live it unconscious of your own divinity? How would you distinguish yourself and your consciousness as the divine self and the consciousness of God compared to a bird, an animal who does not have the same chance to remember itself and to recognize its consciousness as a divine being?

There is a burden of responsibility that has been given to you alongside of the divine benefit of knowing that you and God are one.

The responsibility is that you have to remain in that oneness and if you have moved away from it, you have to return to it. The benefit is that in that divinity, you are living life in oneness. What good is life if you don't live it in oneness?

Why then waste a human body, mind, emotions, spirit and soul if you were to live in ignorance of that fact that you are a divine and holy being of light walking upon Earth as the illumination of God's light. If you are to choose to continue to live in ignorance of this bliss, then why waste a human body? Come as a bird. Come as a fish. Come as a wild animal. Because even your pets have the consciousness and the knowing that they are divine holy beings of light. [Wild animals, unlike pets, are unconscious of their divinity.]

The presence of the Seven Mighty Elohim and our accelerated participation in your life is for the purpose of achieving a greater knowledge and remembrance that you are divine holy beings of light, emanations of God's heart sparks. And that God has intended for you to remember your true origin. We come to you to remind you.

In this process, we offer you a remembrance and all the assistance that is needed for the process of remembering to complete itself.

In return, you become responsible the moment you agree to remember, to focus all the attention on attaining the final goal of mastering ascension, returning to the divine heart core of God as the sparks that you are, remembering that you are those sparks and letting go of the ignorance and the forgetfulness of this fact. We bring this message and all the assistance required to attain this final goal. As you receive us, as you open your heart to us, we will assist you in manners that you have not even thought of, in ways you would consider miraculous.

In return, we ask that you take responsibility for that remembrance and that you act accordingly, acting as conscious, responsible, divine human sparks of light who remember that their true origin belongs to the heart of God.

In the cosmic light that is emanated from the heart of the Most High, I stand illuminating light to all of you. I am Elohim Hercules representing the Seven Mighty Elohim and the Sevenfold Flame of Elohim Light.

Grid of Light to Anchor the Energies of Peace, Purity, Truth, Love, Power, Wisdom and Unity

Elohim Hercules, channeled July 11, 2003

Our presence will become more prominent in time until together we will raise the vibration of Earth and the consciousness of humanity to a level where with every breath, every soul of this planet will call to reunite in God as God.

Beloveds, I am Hercules. My essence here on Earth is to bring you wisdom and knowledge. The lineage of light from which I come forth is the cosmic essence of the Elohim.

I bring to you from my own heart flame the pure light of the Seven-Fold Flame, which started the entire manifestation process from the Great Void, manifestation as God in form.

In the presence of the I Am That I Am, I open my heart and I offer to you a grid of light, in the name of peace, in the name of purity, in the name of truth, in the name of love, in the name of power, in the name of wisdom, in the name of unity. I bring you the Seven-Fold Flame to anchor the energies of the qualities I have just given to you.

- Find a white candle for each quality. Imbue [that is, empower with your will] the candle with that quality—peace, purity, wisdom, love, truth, unity, and divine power. You should have eight candles, seven for each of the qualities that I have mentioned, and one for the Seven-Fold Flame.

- Place a white sheet of paper, preferably cut in the form of a circle, under your candle grid.

• Find the herbal essence of valerian root and rub that essence on every one of the candles. Immerse a white circular sheet of paper into the valerian root herbal essence, almost as though you have soaked it, and let it dry.

• In the center of that circle write the intention that you would like to manifest.

• Place the paper under the candles.

• Place a clear glass, round shaped jar filled with water directly over the intention that you have written in the center of the paper.

• Light the candles every day until that intention has been attained.

• As you light each candle, invoke those qualities. You may choose to write those qualities on the outside of the circle where you place your candles so that you would repeat the same quality for the same candle each time.

• At the end of calling to the qualities, call upon the Seven Mighty Elohim of Creation, the Seven-Fold Flame of Creation and the presence of the I Am That I Am.

• Imbue each candle and each quality. Furthermore, imbue the intention that you have set this grid for. Every day fill your grid with love from your heart, with the joy of knowing that your intention has already been granted and that it will come to the manifest form through the force and the power of light and the love that you put into it.

Because you live in a linear time-space continuum, it might take a short span of time for the full manifestation process to complete itself. [That is, the process may not be instantaneous.]

Be patient. Don't lose your joy. Don't give up on the love. Those are the two most important elements. Your love and joy for manifesting the intentions is as important as the invocation of the Elohim and the invocation to the presence of the I Am.

The one final element that will manifest any event and bring it into your realm of reality is the love and joy you imbue it with.

We are always present in your world and in ours. Our presence does not go away. What prevents you from manifesting the objects of your desires is the love and the joy that need to go into the process.

Your love and your joy are the breath of life that you breathe into each event to bring it into this level of existence.

If you don't breathe the breath of light and life into an object, it will remain dormant. It will remain lifeless. For it to come to life, it needs to breathe. For it to begin breathing, it needs to receive the breath of life through the love and joy that you place into it.

It really is as simple as that. The moment that you loose your love and your joy, even if it is an instant before the manifestation, the lights go out, and you go back into dormancy and the event is put on hold. The moment you turn on the lights by turning your love and joy back on, it comes to life again. When you continue to pour out love and joy, you will achieve the object of your desires faster.

Perseverance and continuity are the second factor. It is important to have the love and the joy. It is also important to continue to maintain the love and the joy until you have attained the object of your desires and not a moment before because even to the penultimate moment before its manifestation, you do not have the object in your hands, in your life, so you don't have the results in manifest form.

So even one moment before its manifestation, it is not good enough for you to claim it [until it has physically manifested]. You can only claim it when you have completed the action and the action has manifested in physical form. Once it is in manifest form, you must continue to breathe the life into it through your love and joy.

Again, if you were to withdraw from pouring out the breath of life into it, it will go into dormancy. What is the benefit of a beautiful new car, after you have manifested it, if it stays in the garage for the rest of its living life and never gets to be driven in joy and in love? This is a simple analogy but an appropriate one.

Continue with the love and the joy for every project that you begin from the beginning to the end.

And even at its ending, bless it and love it and fill it with joy so that even the closure of that chapter, even the completion of that book, even if it is the book of life, be a joyful and loving experience.

If you begin a project [such as this grid], you never stop until that project has come to fruition. When you stop for an extended period of time, you deflate whatever energies you have built up and that means you have to start all over again to rebuild the energy. You can get faster momentum but you can never stop until you have achieved the objects of your desires.

In the same way that you have the discipline of eating as many times a day, a week, a month, in the same way that you have the discipline of washing your body, brushing your teeth, you must gain the discipline of learning that whatever you take upon yourself, you see it through its completion and not a moment before.

If you stop a project the moment before its manifestation, it doesn't manifest, even if it is one second before its manifestation. When a baby is born through a birth canal, there's always that last push. If you don't give that last push, what happens? The baby eventually comes out but dead, stillborn.

Do not give your power to one person or another.

Your power is in remembering that you are God. Your power is in remembering that for as long as you have recognized yourself as God, God walks by your side. Your power is in remembering and recognizing that God knows best and God wants the best for all of you. For you are each fragments of God's being-ness.

For as long as you cannot believe in the God within you to be able to conduct your needs and your desires to the fullest, you will not allow the God within you to do just that-- you will stand in your own way of attaining the objects of your desires.

You would live in mistrust of the God that runs your life. You would be commanding that God to drive your car to somewhere safe without handing that God the keys to the car.

And that's what you all do on a daily basis. You issue decrees and give commands without fully embracing the commandments and the decrees and then you say: No one has heard me. I wonder if God is really there listening to me.

Those are statements made on a daily basis. The true statement should have been: Thank you, God, that you have already heard my needs and have taken care of them. I know that on this day, just as on any other day, I would be taken care of, and to trust that it will be done and to call with every breath upon the presence of God in the form of the blessed presence of the I Am That I Am.

The most important thing in remembering and realizing that you are God and God is within you is to recognize the presence of the I Am That I Am.

I Am That I Am is that aspect of God that has taken form, moved into action, released itself from the Great Void to manifest form, knows the meaning and the essence of being in manifest form, knows your plight and knows how to rescue you from your pain and suffering— but will not do it unless you ask to be rescued because this planet is about having free will.

You, as representatives of humankind, chose this plight and brought it upon yourselves by saying: Okay, God, I know how to do it. Let me go out and do it. Let us do it my way this time.

And God, in loving you, chose to let you do it your way. For as long as you continue to want to do it your way, you will not be interceded or interfered with. It is only when you choose to ask for intercession that assistance will come.

It is only when you offer your own will and align it with the will of God I Am that you will receive direct guidance from the Source.

And until then, you have got to practice with every breath to realign your will with the will of God I Am, until you no longer distinguish between the breath that you take and the breath of God. Because originally you came from that breath of God. You were created from the winds of God's breath, pushed and pulled into the surface of existence and back again.

It is a simple analogy but a very important one. Once you fully understand this analogy, you will have attained your mastery and you return to your own essence as divine holy beings that recognize themselves as God and live in oneness in God.

Energies of the Seven Mighty Elohim of Creation are being lowered upon Earth right now.

My own presence as Hercules is to be taken as the representation and spokesperson for the Seven-Fold Flame and the Seven Mighty Elohim. Our presence will become more prominent in time until together we will raise the vibration of Earth and the consciousness of humanity to a level where with every breath, every soul of this planet will call to reunite in God as God.

At that point, mass ascension is achieved and your planet will begin the completion of its rebirthing process. The completion of this rebirthing process means that your planet and all the souls would have ascended to the level of higher beings of light. The planet and the souls from this present density that you experience as your third dimensional reality would be removed; they would enter into higher realms of light, orbiting differently. The quality and texture of time-space will be different in those realms of light.

The light itself will have a more liquid and fluid substance to it at those levels. The experience could be assimilated with the analogy of doing aerobics exercises— standing on Earth and moving your body in the air, or doing aerobic exercises standing in a body of water and moving your body in the water. In the water, your body weighs much less. The movement becomes easier in the water compared to the air.

The same applies to higher levels of light, and dimensions and realms of ascension. You would be moving in higher intensities of light, which will make the movement easier compared to what you experience in this present reality. In the same way, pain and suffering will not have such a grip on you as it does in this present reality. Emotions have no need of running rampant. The mind does not play games with you any longer, and the body will have a much easier function and less of a burden.

This is the final object of all exercises, the final conclusion of being in human physical embodiment for all souls, including the planet and the solar system, the galaxy and so forth— until all returns into its all-ness in the heart core of All That Is. All that has come into physical manifest material form returns into non-matter, non-manifest light— vibration, in oneness.

Divine Mother

The Divine Mother is the epitome of the creative force of the universe. She is the feminine principle of existence. She holds the womb of the Earth within her own being; therefore, all fertility and procreativity are hers.

All the goddesses and all other feminine beings are aspects or drops from the ocean that the Divine Mother is. The Hindus consider Goddess Kali as the Divine Mother; Christians consider the Virgin Mary or Mother Mary as the Divine Mother. But while Kali and Mother Mary are unquestionably divine mothers, the Divine Mother we refer to here is the absolute divinity who is beyond form because her energy is so vast.

I have channeled the energies of the Divine Mother but I have never channeled her speaking through me. I suspect that if I did, my circuits would burst. In my experience, I see the Divine Mother as the silhouette of a female inside tongues of fire. Her voice is like the sound of rumbling water. Yet her energy is as smooth and as soft as silk.

My first encounter with the Divine Mother was many years ago. I have learned to call upon her in times of extreme distress. Recently, when I called on her while meditating, she appeared to me as a silhouette in red flames and she gently told me to finish the work I needed to do and then return to meditate at 1 pm.

As it turned out, I got very busy and I didn't get back to my meditation until 3 pm. When I did, the Divine Mother made a brief appearance and told me that I had missed my chance because I had missed the appointed hour of 1 pm.

I was quite surprised to hear this. I had misinterpreted her gentle ways. I figured she would understand my being late just as my mother did when I was a child and just as I have done with my own child. It was only a few hours, after all. But of course this was the Divine Mother and she had a point to make. She was teaching me obedience and humility.

When I got over my amazement at being rejected, I decided to somehow get the Divine Mother to forgive me. I told her that I would sit in meditation and repeat her name for as long as it took for her to forgive me. I sat upright all night in meditation. Around 6 am (I was watching the time very closely!) the next morning, the Divine Mother finally appeared to me. She said that I had learned my lesson and she accepted my apology.

The following passage— Merging with the Energies of the Divine Mother— is spoken by Metatron who is delivering the energies of the Divine Mother. That is, she is "appearing" through Metatron. Before you read, prepare yourself to enter into sacred communion with the highest feminine principle of existence. When you have finished, take a deep breath and sit still for a few moments to absorb the energies.

Merging with the Energies of the Divine Mother

Metatron, channeled July 28, 2002

Take a deep breath with me. Become aware of the presence of the Goddess, the feminine principle, the Divine Mother energies.

I request on your behalf that the Divine Mother will stand in front of you and allow you to step into her energies by becoming one with her and merging your energies with hers.

From this merging you will receive a greater focus, will-fullness, hope, and the love to stand in the truth of God's love. It is the truth of God's love that I request on your behalf to be given to you, as you step into her energy field and merge as one with her.

Take a deep breath and envision yourself standing in front of the Divine Mother. Feel her energies emanating to you. Say a prayer of thanksgiving for this encounter. Visualize yourself stepping into her energy field and merging with her being. Fill your lungs with her presence. Fill your heart with the emanations of love from her heart.

Listen. See if you can hear her words, if you can see her, if you can feel her presence. If you can hear her words, receive your message. Otherwise, stay for a few minutes and pray that she will make her presence known to you in your life in whatever way she sees fit.

Take a deep breath. Let us together pray and thank the blessed presence of the Divine Mother and the healing energies that we have received from her.

Repeat this meditation regularly to benefit from the presence and the essence of the feminine principle of existence, the Divine Mother in your being and your life.

We thank the Divine Mother energies for this blessing.

Acknowledgements

We thank all the beings of light who participated in this volume and allowed us to bring their teachings to you. We pray that their blessings reach all across our beloved Mother Earth and beyond. It is our hope that through the channeled discourses in this book, our readers will feel the indescribable love that we feel when an ascended being of light comes through.

Denise Kahn and Kathleen Speers, thank you for joining our team in creating this book. We could not have done it without you. Thank you, Kathy, for lending your talent to the design, typography and formatting. Thank you, Denise, for all the many things you had a hand in, not least reading the manuscript and suggesting changes.

Thanks also to Melania for reading. Thanks to Michael Kopel and Toni Maria Range Pinhiero for transcribing tapes, and Michael for helping with a misbehaving computer.

Thanks to Noosheen Safai Tavakoli and family for their help with Persian and Islamic literature.

Thanks to Karen Sunde for her prompt assistance on such short notice.

Thanks to the hermit priest Father John of the Trinity for his special prayers.

Thanks to Dr. John Alderson for his loving support.

Thanks to all those, including Fritz and Daisy, who participated in these channelings, whether in private sessions, ceremonies or workshops.

Thanks also to Shelley Sapyta at BookMasters for her wise, patient directions.

We are blessed to have the love and light of you all.